Inside the Heart of

Kevin Begos

By: Rose Griffin

In Loving Memory of My Dear Friend, Author, Scientist, Award Winning Journalist, Mayor, Kevin Paul Begos Jr, Thank You For Dancing The Dance Of Friendship, Love And Laughter With Me…. May You Forever Rest In Peace And Never Be Forgotten. (2021)

My Truth and Gratitude,

I oftentimes write and am very proud of my gift, I consider myself avid and straightforward, But, in coming to terms with this situation of death and being able to dig deep inside myself, this was the most challenging time of my life. This book almost lost itself in my private heart, the challenge that loomed inside of me, as to whether people should see my personal life almost took center stage. So, I give thanks to my daughter Trinity and son in law Johnathan, for their countless hours of love, support and a shoulder to cry and lean on, for pushing me to share Kevin's Truths.

Thank You Kids

Table Of Content

The Pearls along the way

I found things of value, like walking along a deserted road trying to make my way to the well of life, I found time, time to grab Pearl's along the way

I found a pail to gather the water, Once I reached my well. I found a small cushioned seat to sit on, while drinking from the well.

I found sweet butter bread to nibble on whilst I sit and rest, while gathering the physical strength I needed, thinking of a plan to carry me pass my well

A small cup of endurance was sitting there too, I guess that will become useful , I found a broken heart, immediately I knew it needed mending so I brought it along too.

I found satisfaction and pushed it down deep inside my pocket, because I knew, only It would be able to satisfy my blues, kiss my forehead and heart too.

I found seeds of birth lying in my womb so to be fruitful I did that too, I found laughter, I grabbed a double dose of that cup too,

I sat at the well and nibbles on my bread, hoping to find a picture of your face imprinted in my head, a glance or two would be all I need, anything to help my journey go with speed.

I now sit at my well and I wonder why? Why you left and did not say goodbye? I guess that wasn't your choice, as I've guessed from this day, because lord know my choice wasn't to be sitting at the well this way.

So yet as I travel, I do it with grace, thinking of all the treasures I've gathered along the way, many were not joyous and yet some gave me glee, but I will travel until I make it to thee. (c) 2020 By Rose Griffin

His Mother, Lady Jane

A soft fragile voice came piercing through the phone, and the words I heard next sent my soul over a cliff "Rose, I knew you would be worried if he was alone, but he wasn't, I held his hand until he passed away." Those were the words of his mother, she is an aged mother, who sat by the bedside of her baby boy holding his hand, as he slipped into the arms of Jesus.

I think I froze, I think I cried, I think I retreated, I think I ……..Died that day, because I had just spoke with him a few days prior and he was coming home, this home, the home we laughed in, the home we made plans in, THE HOME.

Chapter 1

The Eulogy

So now what!

He's dead, he's gone, just like that, one days he's planning on running a city and the next he is in a morgue. "There will be no next" ......I'm standing here looking out upon all these people, some I know and some I have never seen before, trying to look composed, prim and proper. Knowing full well, that at any moment, my legs could fall from underneath me and the whole world would know that I am a fake, that I am not composed, that I am not the epidemy of grace, that my smile is plastered on, only by the grace of god. That, at any moment now, I may fall flat on my face and never get up again, I can't see, I can't feel, I can't breathe, I can't believe, I am a shell, I am a frozen Ice Princess, who has been appointed to say the last words, over someone she thought would be around for 50 more years, in laughter and debate.

So now here I stand, Lord Please Let Me Stand one more time for him, this has been a very hard and emotional time, I saw so much hatred, as if they were waiting for him to die (it seems as if they had him buried even before he died and had his seat already re-assigned out). Those that I expected to show up at his Memorial, as I look out into the audience, are nowhere to be found. So yes, Lord please let me stand.

Secretly all kinds of obstacles presented themselves, as in a last-ditch effort to diminish who he was, or to get the last laugh. It seemed as if all the things his sister and I tried, were met with sheer viper venom, the spikes were out, and they weren't being masked, they were full-fledged visible. Which in turn sent me in a superhero spiral, pledging to keep it together, even if it was the last thing I did. Cassandra and I was going to pull this off and we did well, with the help of a few devoted friends, we mustered up enough support to stand and send him away in style.

My nerves were in my stomach, it felt as if labor pains were engulfing every nerve I owned, they are expecting me to have the answer, but I don't. I felt a separation of something deep inside my soul that shook my entire being. I felt a pull, as if something deep inside of me was shook to the very core. I was thinking, after this memorial stuff was over, I could get myself together, I will be in peace, I will get into my bed and feel what seems to be gone, I had lost my taste, my smell, I could barely hear, I walked around waiting to lay down. I wanted to cry, but as soon as I felt tears forming between my eyes, the phone would ring, or someone would need me for something. Or there was something wrong and I needed to fix it.

I channeled my peace, because It was all in the name of making sure Kevin's last walk, would not be clouded in anything but perfection, and that it was, the troops rallied around and off we went, I think the crowning part was hearing John Solomon's voice every day, he is the Director of the Apalachicola Bay Chamber of Commerce and Director of the Tourist Development Council, my former boss and dear friend, as he did call, text or email me daily just to say, "you're going to be just fine, just take deep breaths and call me if you need me".

I took a deep breath,

 cleared my throat,

stepped up to the podium and said;

He was known for traveling the world ,
He studied Science at Bards, law and so many other things
He received the Arab Science Journalist Award,
He reported for the Associated Press and the Winston Salem Journal,
He wrote books, alone and in conjunction with others,
He sat in Monasteries and learned from Monks,
He owned two book publishing companies,
And might i add, as icing on the cake, he was also elected Mayor by THE PEOPLE of the City of Apalachicola.
These facts I've just spoken of, can be found in any Google search, under the hand of any person whom desired to check.

   Therefore, I am not here today to discuss Mayor Begos, the Journalist, the Author nor the Scientist. I am here because of my Friend, the "Man"

   As I stand before you today, I believe I have earned the privilege and right to bear witness to the brilliance of whom Kevin was and his earthly desires, along with his deep determination to bring our community into a place of legitimacy and pride. While baring witness to his soul, as it opened unto the dawn of generosity and peace, as it enveloped the characteristics of this community and its people. I sat in the presence of his power, watched him gently take on many forms and directions, as he enveloped the vows he had taken to guard, defend and protect this City as a Man, Friend and a Mayor.

Being Kevin's friend meant dealing with layers, shields and decades of things that had plagued him as a human man, things that had broken his spirit and hurt his feelings, but also ignited passions no one could ever begin to imagine. I was blessed and honored to have been his friend, whether it was 7:45 in the morning, he would say let's meet for breakfast or a phone call at 2 am, where something from earlier that day or week had crushed or confused him and he was just THEN, beginning to feel the effects of that situation and needed to release himself of those heart wrenching burdens. Sometimes he just wanted to hear a voice that was not surrounded in condemnation and judgement.

Generally, the practice is to stand before man and proclaim the dead as superior, well-adjusted being with no faults. That is what happens, when some people die, the eulogist, the family and friend, sometimes tries to rebuild the dead person character, whether that was the truth or not. I am very grateful, my friend doesn't require such rebuilding, because his life and legacy spoke for its self,
His love spoke for itself,
His kindness spoke for its self,
His heart spoke for its self,
His merit stood bright,
His conditioning stood steadfast,

His intellect has been mass produced and sold all around the world.

I am so grateful today, that when God was looking for true fruit to place on the tree of Apalachicola, he chose Kevin. Although his Mayoral term was cut short, his legacy has a resounding effect, that will be remembered, wished for and observed for decades to come, because his fruit/ his deeds spoke for themselves.

In closing I would leave you with what I call Kevin's favorite words:

I learned of his love for these words, after an encounter I witnessed where someone had deliberately tried to demean his character.

I later loudly said, "well I know you're not going to just keep standing still while people walk all over you in disrespect".

He smiled and said "Calm down Rose", I knew the dangers when I asked for this position, I knew that the true selves (fruit) of men and women would surface. But that has nothing to do with what I have decided to do.

And then he reached inside an old book, which was place on a small table next to his couch, (a table I would later learn was built by his departed father), took out a small page handed it to me, a very small piece of paper as of ancient texture, it looked as if it had been traveled and worn, used and lived by. And it read:

And another also said, Lord, I will follow thee; but let me first go bid them farewell, which are at home, at my house. And Jesus said unto him, no man, having put his

hand to the plough, and looking back, is fit for the kingdom
of God.

I smiled, because I knew he was a jewel amongst jewels.
I knew that he had placed his hand to a plough and
regardless to what was ahead or behind him, he would
never deliberately release that plough,
he would never let go of the charge he had to keep, or look
back in regret, because his fruits, his character nor his
deeds would allow such.

Chapter 2

The Watchful Eye

(Phone rings) Hello Girl, yes, I called you, I just wanted to tell you something. Now don't think I'm crazy or being overly suspicious, But I swear someone is following me, well maybe not following me, but have you ever seen the same car or the same person 8 times in one week? I have and its creepy, anyway I don't know who he is, he's rather friendly, smiles a lot and has openly spoken and acknowledged my presence, whether at the gas station, grocery store, the Island or just in passing.

No, I don't know who he is, I said that already. I have no earthly idea who he is, but I can say his voice is very pleasant and you can just tell he's probably kind, simple looking guy, no flashy points at all. Simple dresser, simple walker, just a regular guy I'm thinking. No, I do not know his name, I never asked, I'm trying to tell you something, stop asking all these questions, I simply wanted you to know what is going on just in case I disappear, that isn't funny, stop laughing. You see, that's why i do not tell you any of my business, you laugh too much. Ok, here's my why? Although this town is small, there is no reason for me to continually see the same person that many times in a week, it's as if they have me bugged or something, like they have a low jack on my car.

Yesssssssss, I'm serious, I am really serious. Maybe he's a tourist or maybe he's some creepy guy with a thick girl fetish, I don't know, but I do know he's been in my visor more than necessary and its beginning to make me paranoid, I just thought I would clue you in, as my friend just in case something happens to me. Here's the color of his car,,,,,,,,, and this is what he looks like,,,,,,,,,,,,,,,. Yes, that is what he looks like, oh so you think that mean he's scoping, lol, any way I gotta go to work, I will call you tonight, answer that phone,

Chapter 3

The Meeting

(about three months later)

I pulled into the Piggly Wiggly parking lot, known to some as the Red Rabbit. "I hate this store" was all I could think to say, as I slammed my car door, you can never find a parking space, the tourist drives me crazy, the locals park crazy and I'm always stuck somewhere in between. Well I'll just run in and run out, I shouldn't even cook, I'm sick of them kids, one of them should be cooking for me.

Would you like me to get that for you? Those words were the only sounds I heard, right before I froze. the voice was so penetrating, so close, so sultry, so deep, so so so inviting, I almost forgot to speak. Slowly I turned around and it was him that Damn stranger, that strange guy from that strange orange car, staring at me with those strange piercing eyes and boy like smile. Just as I began to say NO, he reached around me grabbed the Penne from the shelf and said, "I think this is the one you really like", Now, how in the Hell did he know? well that's exactly what I wanted to know and say, but I froze.

With outstretched hands and a wide opened mouth, I grabbed the Penne from his long arm and wide hand, I thanked him and headed straight for the register, totally forgetting all the other ingredients I came there for. I paid, ran to my car, sat there and waited for my heart to jump out my pocket and back into my chest. Normally this would not be a point of fear, but because I had already assumed this guy was following me, Today I became totally convinced, not to mention he knew which pasta I liked, why, how, when, what, I am now without a doubt, the owner of a stalker. Well I don't have time for all of this, who was he and why is he and where did he come from? I better get answers.

(I better call my Boss), he knows everybody, he will know who this creep-o is, for sure. Where is my phone? Hey Guy!!!!! Guess what I think I'm being stalked, (laughter) no seriously, there is this man, I've seen him at least 8 times in a week, I pulled up to the gas pump he pulled up, I went to the store, he ended up in the store, I went to the restaurant, within minutes so was he, and today I was trying to find some pasta he picked up the Penne and said it was my favorite. I am sitting in my car scared stiff.

Well this is what he looks like.......... And his car is this color...... What's funny? Do you know him or not? You are right, there are hundreds of white men with that very same description, but, no I don't, what's his name? that's why I called you, I thought you knew everybody, and yes, he does look like he's a somebody.

(Good morning, have you seen your stalker today? Says the boss with the jokey jokes)
No, I have not and that's why I don't tell you anything, because you think everything is a joke,,,,, We are going on the other side for lunch, can you watch the front for about 30 minutes. I hadn't no longer sat down and picked up my fork to eat, when the door to the office opened, as the doorbell chimed so did the voice, and all I heard was;

(about 6 months later)
Hello, Good morning My name is...... are you the Director, is all I heard? My God that was the voice!!!!!!!!, that was the man, that was the stranger, that was the stalker, that was the point of my total paranoia. I cannot believe this, I just cannot! How did he find me? Maybe that's not him, my coworker looked at me and said, Damn what is wrong with you? I asked her, do you not hear that? she said

what? I said that voice! Don't you hear that? ohhhhh my god!!!! Who is that. (At this point my curiosity had swallowed my inner common sense and because the office wall divider was extremely high, therefore, in order to see his face, I would need to climb on top of the desk and peer over to the other side, Which I did.

The top of his head was all I saw, I climbed down, disappointed, my coworker Samantha said, who in the Hell is that Anyway? and why are you freaking out? I told her the story about the voice, the encounters, the store, the gas pump, the smile and the eyes. She smiled and said You Go Girl!!!, well for me, that was not a "you go girl" moment, not at all, it was a crazy time and I had no control over it.

Somewhere within the next couple weeks, he showed back up again and this time I was front and center, he walked in and said good morning, copped a squat right next to me. I had no escape, I had to sit there and pretend my heart hadn't dropped on the floor, he talked to my boss who sat there with this Cheshire Cat grin, loving every minute of my panic attack, basking in the glory that something had rocked my pedestal and almost knocked me off my perch. I watched my boss skillfully ask him question, delving deep into his world, making sure we knew the things I was dying to know (Thanks Boss, Good Looking Out).

Finally, without skipping a beat, he turned to me smiled and said hello I am Kevin, is there something you would like to know about me (with an outstretched hand, waiting for a handshake). (Nope I did not shake his hand) But instead, I looked him square in the face and said; Well yeah, first of all, where did you get them dreamy eyes and sexy voice, "Noooooo I did not say that", I cleared my throat and went straight for the jugular, so you're the man running for Mayor? So why have I not seen you Campaigning on the Hill (which is a predominantly African American Neighborhood), do you suppose you're to good to bring yourself up there? He laughed so loud and said no ma'am, I just assumed they had found a person and it would be useless or disrespectful, I did not want to do that.

I again attacked, so are you saying, those people do not have the intellect to deal with more than one candidate, or to make an informed decision? or do you assume because they are black, they are going to vote for another person just because they are black also? Do you see us as that? With you being white, would you vote for someone just because they are white? He said no I would not, I then said ok, well I guess I can expect to see you out and about, voicing your desired plans for my community and my people? I am assuming this conversation means "we" you and I, have set a standard right? He smiled again and said yes ma'am we surely have (with the most fascinating smirk on his face). He stood up, began to walk out, he turned around and said can I call you, I said yes sir you surely can.

Chapter 4

The Arm

(about 9 months later)

That was such an amazing dinner, classy, sassy and fun. The conversation educating, as the evening stars shone bright, the fragrance of patchouli filled the air and I felt blessed, without a single word, his arm circled around my shoulder and all was right with the world. I took a deep breath and I kept walking. Not in a million years or a million words would I ever reveal the intense fear that enveloped my inner being, nothing and I mean nothing had ever frightened me as did that arm, as it gently rested on my shoulder. In that moment I lost all conscience and I retreated back to the little girl, who found peace in simple acts of kindness, but at the same time, she, that little girl had an excited feeling, that this was the beginning of much more than anything she had planned for.

Who am I kidding I was frighten as could be, dang it, what the hell was going on, I hope he's not thinking what I think he's thinking, I am not doing that. Oh My Goodness, Please Lord Please let this man calm down, why is his arm around me and why am I so frightened, this is moving wayyyyyyy to fast. I almost jumped out of my skin, I looked around for a reason to ask him to remove his arm and there was none. So, I smiled and kept walking. All the while holding my breath, because that arm felt so peaceful, so secure and so right. It was a point of pride for me to abstain from any emotional attachments, as I knew full well those type actions and emotional attachments could only lead to tragedy, as they always did. But I looked up at him smiled and soaked in the newness of it all. His gentle strides felt freeing, they reminded me of a gallant gentle giant lurking over me in a protective manner and as my heart softly began to open, I felt peace. Peacefully walking with someone's arm around me, no words just walking, soaking in the refreshing air and letting our new friendship speak for itself.

As we walked, every so often I could hear his breath as it moved slowly and deliberately, as if he was attuned to the earth that lingered under his feet, as if being there was natural and a needed desire as normal as putting on his shoes or as normal as the oxygen that penetrated the earth, something so needed and something without warning had captured our essence and sent us on a world wind of unconscious meetings of the minds, hearts and souls. Such a real feeling, droplets of the fresh air touched my skin, as if an open door from afar had made its way into our atmosphere, a newness was blooming right before our very eyes, so quietly we walked, while our souls became friends once again.

Chapter 5

The Conversation

(1 year,4 days and 26 minutes)

Hello Rose, are you busy today, can we have a conversation this afternoon? (he was so polite in his invitations, almost sterile) Hello, yes, we can. I will stop by your house around 7. He said meet me at the Chinese Restaurant, afterward we will go back to my house. At this point, meeting him had become a regular occurrence and I found those times to be noteworthy, exciting and I prepared myself for the intrigue of the conversation and debates.

After dinner we retreated to his home, a very simple place, with an urgent hint of intellect and history making items, a place in which a man of study would call home, a place where simply things, with no frills were visible. As I walked through the door, the smell of welcome mixed with manly rustic cologne enveloped my nostrils, bringing my senses yet again ablaze. The funniest thing is, each encounter I found myself in with this man, was an encounter of an ahh hah moments, I became engrossed in our time as a kid waiting for Christmas, not because of some sexual exploits, but because I never left him unlearned, and was always impressed with our meeting.

I sat in a very stylish chair which sat close to a window, I had found that to sit there, I was most comfortable and that particular chair made me feel as if I was sitting on a throne and he was my subject, he was the one who listened intently and contently, he was the one who ordered my knowledge with expertise, sitting with him was as if providence was at work and my gifts and talents were being oiled, shaped, and set to mastership.

He smiled then offered me a drink of Mango Punch, a drink I offered him the first time he came to my house for dinner, he had never tasted mango punch before, so each time thereafter, we treated each other with Mango Punch (a special treat which I learned to make, from my elderly neighbor and children's babysitter in Orlando, A beautiful Haitian lady, by the name of Jeanine Basile), this was our secret special treat which meant something to our encounters, it said here you are, this is something only we share, something that connects us in solidarity and friendship, something that no one had privilege or knowledge of, just us two, our island in the middle of this crazy world, our place of connection. Our peace offering, our kiss of friendship, our bond.

He sat near me, he started off with there is a lot I want to tell you, but that is for another time, (Secretly I hated that statement, he always said that, I wanted to know then, not later, because I am very nosey mixed with curiosity, but I smiled and said ok) he then went on to tell me a story about his life and his encounters with women, "his not so good" track record in relationship. He leaned in and said, I'm not one who would blame the women for all my failures, I'm sure being a journalist, traveling from state to state, town to town, borough to borough, parish to parish, it just became too much for them. So, I guess it was just as much my fault as it was theirs.

No one wants to wait around for other people to complete their task, I felt so sorry for him, the look on his face was as if, he was a little child confused and full of fear. I felt so sad in my heart, because my heart heard his plea of reservation and hurt, I'm sure there had been that special person the one or even more than one, whom he assumed he would spend the rest of his life with and yet, it all came crumbling at his feet, simply because he enjoyed working. Simply because his craft took him from place to place, simply because the balance between work and love had no space, or simply because love had no time.

After what seemed like hours of sharing secrets, telling each other of private things, things we had not shared with anyone else, things we held sacred and things we only thought god knew, we opened our hearts and poured out our inner most beings to each other, without any fear, without any shame, without any reservations, in that moment I knew I had finally met my true friend for life, my soul partner, my buddy, my secret sharer, my ride or die, my only ally and my lean on me when you are not strong.

Finally with permission to trust each other, laying our cards on the table, we knew being near each other was where we were meant to be, but we also decided that we would not put pressure on each other, we would not ask more from each other than what we were openly ready to give, we decided to keep each other's secrets, keep each other's friendship, keep each other's respect, keep each other choices to live without obligation. We made a deal that at that point, we would not demand anything extra

27

from one another, but that we would keep ourselves open for ours friendship.

We sat there staring at each other in amazement, finally he laughed and said, WOW, we are a pair of misfits, aren't we? I shook my head because I knew he was right, although we did not say all we were feeling or all we had intended to, we did say enough, we both knew we were meant to have met, we were meant to have shared, it was meant for us to sit there across from each other, knowing full well, all was well with our souls and all would be well with us.

After that long conversation, a few weeks later we had decided to go on our first and official date, everything before that was just hanging out!!!!! We are heading out to enjoy each other's company. I wonder where we will end up, it is so exciting, I haven't been on a date in almost two decades, LOL this is giddy and scary at the same time. My mind continuously flows back to what will be expected of me, how will I respond, what will I say and how will he handle the rejection, because for sure anything physical is off the table, although he's very charming, I truly am not ready for that.

Not to say he's anything but a perfect gentleman, I assume this topic of conversation will eventually arise and would need to be dealt with, I'm in between a rock and a hard place, I'm not 16 or 21, this is my first friendship in almost 2 decades and I'm scared of messing it up. And I know me, so yes, I could mess it up, I've been so free, for so long, no one to answer to, no one to be accountable to, but God and my Kids, so right now my independence flag fly's very high and proud.

Anyway, we are off to see the wizard so to speak!!!!! This place is so quiet and romantic, beautiful grass, no sounds except water and whistling of trees and splashing waves as they hit the sides of the barrier walls. We are having an old-fashioned picnic,(Well I just be, can you believe this, this guy is actually courting me, the old fashioned way, Bravo to you, Bravo to me) wow a picnic, with sandwiches and dessert from Café Con Leche in Apalachicola, a fancy bistro style cafe, Mango Punch from my recipe, (I taught him how to make it, he's really good at it) he's having wine, something he has on reserve for special occasions. He adored the Coenobium Ruscum "orange" made from Malvasia and two other grapes, as he proudly sipped and schooled me on the art of wine making, tasting and savoring.

As he peeled back the covering of the picnic basket, he spoke of the food and the owner of Café Con Leche (Tamara), he spoke of his friendship with her and how she welcomed him into this town, made sure he felt at home, invited him to events, he felt that they had a warm and trustful friendship. He smiled as he recounted his getting to know her and her family. He offered me food, drink and truthful conversation, we laughed, he read to me from his novel "Tasting The Past", as we lounged on a red and black striped blanket, which apparently had traveled to distant lands with him throughout the years.

Finally, freedom to breath, finally a friendship that transcended time space and frugality, just two adults with a need for companionship and a truthful, unyielding, no rejections, peaceful environment. As the pages flipped so did his tone, there were times when his words leaped off the pages, and then there were points when a sullen voice surrounded me, as he recounted his time abroad and the adventures of travel. I could tell from his mastery skill with words, he truly enjoyed travel and putting pen to paper. I leaned in closer as the excitement built, the art of travel, the art of making wine, the families, the history and the sheer freedom he had traveling, finding wine and finding himself all while finding peace.

He loved life, his boyish smile spoke volumes, he sat the book down and began to delve into his stories of tasting wines, some good, some not so good, I think his true love was the people in those stories, the lives, the connections, the antics, the generations of pride and togetherness, the kind he had craved and wanted to experience. All the while connecting with generations of knowledge and magic, I guess one could say the scientist in him always became fascinated with the cultivating, fermenting and aging process of those fabulous mouthwatering blends and the total togetherness of mind, body and spirit it took to stand still and trust the process.

As I laid there, soaking in the non-judgement atmosphere, the sheer delight of friendship and the peace of connectivity, I decided in my trust that I would always be his friend, I promised myself that I would have his back, invite him into my world, my friends, my family and my life. I knew from that moment, he would be a person to trust, he would be the one to benefit from the excitement of dinner tables, regular folks, and keen conversation. A place where he would wash away the cares of this world, a non-confrontational atmosphere, where no one was trying to outbid the other, a place where fake forums did not exist. A place to rest his ever-changing brain functions and wash away the blues.

Chapter 6

The Mayoralship

(whose counting)

The video chat chimed in around 2 am, he was still excited, as if his red shiny bike appeared under the tree early on Christmas morning.

Can you believe it, He's a bona fide politician? The smile on his goofy face was priceless, "not in a million years did he think it would happen", was his exact words. But, he had prayed he would get the opportunity, to help the town he had grown to love with his soul. Over thirty years ago, he waltzed into town with all the intention of living a simple, quiet, Journalistic life.

The road to this dream was surely paved in heated hardships. I saw so many daggers stabbing not only him, but other candidates directly in the face, the sight of the malice almost made me lose my taste for people, the art of politics is a game and good spade card player could see that, but the deviousness of the hearts of people is what killed it for me. To stand in the background and observe so many ill-informed people panic, gossip, and make no sense at all, was truly laughable but also downright scary. He dealt with those greedy, self-absorbed, underhanded kind, right from the first day, I kind of felt sorry for him, but it wasn't my race and if I had anything to do with it, (Well you know)

His dream involved travel, investigations, revelations, truth, passion and humanity, not one time did he ever think about politics, Until it was revealed, that in order to be his brothers keepers, he had to get in the game, standing on the sidelines cheering for the underdog, never or very rarely accomplished much, after examining ways to achieve those things, he discovered running for office may be the key. The race of a lifetime, the hustle and agony of teeth clawing his skin and daggers piercing his heart and back, was how he described the sorrow he felt, as he set out to achieve this dream.

With the mind and heart of a child, he assumed his deepest desires could be met by trust and hard work, all to fall flat on his face as he sank deeper in disbelief, disbelief that the community members, those of generational supposed pride, was the very ones destroying the essence of what their forefathers had used blood, sweat and tears to keep. This was a disastrous source of shame and disgust, as he pondered his being, wondering how the wealth of a land which was passed on through seasons, could be so deliberately given away and dismissed as it was dis-guarded as a piece of tissue that was once used to wipe a flu infected nose.

His approach was to soothe the conscience of man, to help them reach a place of pride, not in money, not in self-centeredness, not in possessions, but in the earthly bounty of natural god given things, such as, fresh air, clean water, an abundance of sea creatures, livestock, green grass, love, laughter and a desire to live harmonious. Those were the things which pricked his heart, those were the things that he found to be challenging, as well as missing from the heart and conscience of the natives of Apalachicola Florida, the once viral community with pride in its people and its growth, the water, its yielding's and mostly the people. Those who punctually showed up daily and nightly to produce what made this town seem prosperous (The Seafood Workers).

He desperately wanted the love of community to return, the helping hand, the urgent desire for humanity, the ability to be their brother's keepers and the no man is left behind attitude. I sometimes would look at him and see something he did not see, I saw the real people not the ones I wish was there, but the actual cold and callous individuals who had implanted themselves in this community, thinking that they had found paradise amongst the heathens, it often bothered me that people would come from near and far, to what they called a beautiful haven, but yet they treated the natives as if they were illiterate and easily swayed. The look upon many of those people faces, once they discover how astute we natives really are was priceless.

No one actually knew how desperately he desired for simplicity, a calm sort of Mayberry RFD, with Andy and Barney guarding the gates, probably as he had witnessed on his many trip abroad, to lands and towns where community, family, generations, loyalty, pride, self-awareness, trustworthiness lived. As pure as the grass and rolling hills, as strong as the mountain tops and as peaceful as the sheep that roamed the hills and valleys. Those were his ideas of paradise, those were the ones he had for a world where the buffalo roamed and love abode in a multitude of ways. Not to say it didn't rain on the just as well as the unjust, but that when it did, people handled it without walking on each other's backs while smiling.

But in the process of this life, he found himself head first in the middle of all sorts of things, newspaper shenanigans, oyster shenanigans, visitor shenanigans, neighbor shenanigans and rumored romantic involvements, that were absolutely false. He would smile even chuckle, when he recounted the sorted detailed of some of the things he was accused of, in the back of my mind, I could see some of it actually gave him undisclosed pride, who wouldn't want to be considered a Casanova, that was a dream come true, for a well-guarded gentleman such as himself. Yes, the twinge of masculinity surged through his pride place, although none of it was true, the thought that he would be considered as such, made him blush in male pride.

So yes sir, he was the new Mayor and come hell or high water, he would stand up for this town and all its citizens, regardless of the fame or lack thereof. He was determined to prove that people were inherently good, all they needed was a reason to feel good and show pride. I loved his enthusiasm he was such a trustworthy believer in folks, I guess I had seen so much of people shit, until I did not have the voice to say anything negative, most times I just smiled and said you're so sweet, I pray it all works out in your favor, I would not dare tell him, he was barking up a tree, where people would sooner chop off their mommas right foot, before they treated each other with dignity, pride and respect.

I guess these feeling came from being a native of this town, set in by several generations, the Great granddaughter of a full-blooded Indian, who tilled the land and made a living for his children, grands and great grands (Mr. Oscar Turrell, was his given name, not really sure of his proper name). I had watched the town go from sugar to shit, although people may say the coming together and everybody living together made a difference, but in my eyes that was never the problem, people always co-mingled. That's wasn't the key, the key was the deterioration of the pride of who we were as a City and the lengths people would go through, to change the perception of our fair town.

Anyway, he was Mayor and I was his friend, so yet again there I stood, in the cusp of an era, with a man who was determined to help usher in the newness of peace, harmony and growth without cracking eggs and as gently as possible. A dreamer, a gentle giant, heart so full of love and wishful thinking and an intellect to match. He would have to be strong to undertake the demons that were headed his way, I worked in a place where most of the times I went unnoticed , so I had the opportunity to hear and see a lot of those very same demons, as they cast their lots against him, those were the times I prayed, his beliefs and desires would be met by the power of god, so that he could withstand the wiles of the enemies and there were many.

The Apalachicola Bay

One of the most productive regions on the earth, not just for seafood but for its other qualities, such as the life span of organisms, a natural habitat spanning much further than any documentation has desired to share. This section of God given earth, did not need cultivating. Is there any doubt that the natural inhabitants (the Indians) or do we doubt, that for a group of people who tilled the land much longer than any other did, not know the oyster, shrimp, fish, alligator, bee hive or moss trees were there? or what they meant as life necessities. Perhaps their ability to market those items were of frugality, in as much as they did not appear to be sellers, just users of the land, to the extent of what they needed at the moments. After close study and using family given information, I gathered that They were nomads, seasonal people. They were similar to a boxer, they used the stick and move method.

Although some were steadfast and cultivated the land for growth, yes to the extent of the value needed to survive. In studying human folk, I guess it is really hard for some to surmise, how those folks could not be greedy, as if how can you people be happy with living life on life terms, taking only what is needed for natural growth and life needs.(some of the earlier settlers found this way to be of a benefit) as a child I remember the seasonal oyster harvesting system, (well I'm sure there was another name for it) but this is what I will call it. This was the process of only taking from an oyster bar of the season, there were summer bars and there were winter bars and no one,

I mean no one, could pluck from the out of season oyster beds. Those gate keepers had some common sense of God's earth and to over exert her would lead to eventual disruption of the natural progression of the land and sea. Now this shows, by where we stand today. I sit around and watch the greedy pay for what they thought was gain, from the foolishly needy, the unaware, the simple minded, those without common sense, those who did not know what they had. But perhaps they knew much more than they were asked about or thought to have known. It is now that the know it all's, are scrambling around trying to find their next fix, like some junkie looking for more drugs.

Perhaps the nomadic Indian people, did know the law of the land after all. Anyway, that was my assignment on the preservation of the eco system and the natural actions taken against our simple undeveloped lands, here in Apalachicola. Dry lands, bay land, and riverbank. As a child I recall, going down town with a bunch of the neighborhood kids, we had a string some chicken necks and a hand-held net. We would lay at the edge of the dock and catch crabs all day. The crabs would nestle on the piling which held the docks up. Hundreds of crabs could be found no farther than the docks edge. Other than the string and chicken pieces we used to catch them.

There was maybe a crab basket or two, which would have been the extent of the contraptions needed or used to catch an exorbitant amount of crabs, for food and recreation. Just laughter and patience and following the law of the land, was all it took. As an adult, I now see how too much activity has disrupted the earth's choices, the species development and their right to produce on their terms. Someone one day decided to abort God's mission of his land, just as with the "towel of babble" they began something that would change the land forever, (Well that is, if God just sat back and let them, as Kevin once boldly said).

Elections

The thing about elections and politics!!! if one opens their eyes wide enough or pull off their rose colored Quay, Versace or 9 Five 50/50 shades, they too will be able to see those people for who some of them truly are.

I recall maybe 6 months after his election, he asked me if i wanted to go to an event, i said I think I will pass on that one, because normally It wasn't one I frequented, I then asked why are you going, he said because I told them almost a year ago that I would be there, the next time they had one. Kevin was a man of his word, he kissed babies before his election and he kissed babies after, he ate foods he hadn't ever tasted before, smiled and gave compliments, he served food and made lunches at the Senior Center, he donated money to help the needy, he visited people, he would just stop by folks house, if he saw them sitting on their front porch, just to ask them how they were doing.

And to think that very same generous guy, was sometimes so on edge, it hindered him from enjoying the simple thing in life and pulled him away from the gigantic moments. For example the day of the Seafood Festival Parade of 2019, he was all set to ride in the parade, his golf cart died on him, he called me, I called John Solomon, john sent someone to his rescue, the look of sheer fear flooded his face, I was praying that he would relax long enough to witness his own blessing, shortly after the parade he came to me at the booth, I smiled and said how was it Mr. Mayor? But to my dismay, he had a sullen look. I said what happened now, he quietly said I don't think they like me.

I was so angry with him, I grabbed his jacket and pulled him close to me, looked him square in the eye and said who cares? He looked so shocked and loss, I said do not let anyone hinder the blessing of this moment, how dare you allow some demon out of hell to ruin this day. He smiled and said thank you, I said no problem, now go shake hands and kiss babies, just don't kiss their mama's or you'll have me to deal with. He laughed and said I will see you soon, I said yes you will Mr. Mayor yes you will. He walked off, and I told my co-worker that I was angry with him but could not say so, because I needed him to look pass the crazies and enjoy his triumphant gain. And at the same time, I felt so sorry for him, he clouded his victory with so much worry and needed desired acceptance of the people.

Chapter 7
The Pressure

Oh My God!!!!!!!! I know you're not going to just stand there and watch people disrespect you as if you're not important, how dare they do that, why do you let them? I'm telling you right now, if you don't shut that shit down, they will continually walk all over you, I'm telling you. Well don't be thinking I am going for that, I promise you I will not. Anyway, what is wrong with them, they are the nastiest folks I've ever seen, and I've seen some doozies. Suddenly that sad look returned to his face and I realized, he was hurting not just because of them, but because of me, he needed me to be patient with him and I sometimes forgot just how sensitive he was.

(I hated folks and wasn't afraid to say it, I did not trust most of them and they knew it and they hated me because I knew it. They were accustomed to fake familiar faces, those who normally played by the same games they did, but not me, I dance by my own drummer, especially the day I discovered I owed no one anything. They weren't the author or finisher of my Faith, Job or Life, they had not gotten me to where I was, they had no part in securing my intellect, they were not a party to my home, business or education. I respected who I respected, simply because I desired too, but no, I owed none of them nothing, they hated that, you could see it in their eyes, they only wanted people who owed them or could not survive without them and that person wasn't me, never have been and never will be). But that look snapped me back into reality.

A reality where I gently reminded him, that he was a great man and I just could not stand the tenacity of some and how they with malice and forethought set out to demean him for no earthly reason, he loved people and he wanted all to be in peace, but he did have his limits. I think his main thing was, that I be the Island he turned too when times became hard or people start to tear him down, he simply wanted me to console him, but being a vocal person, I normally did it backwards, after chewing them out, only then would I reach in to say there, there too him. He became familiar with my pattern, I think he sometimes did it just to get a rise out of me and I sometimes said nothing, just to see if he would defend himself.

Once after I went on a rant of people's disrespect toward him he sat near me and gently as always, using his favorite line. "Calm Down Rose" he reached for another book (from that same table near the window) and he pulled out another piece of parchment, so pretty, so delicate this one was of colored texture, which looked as if it had survived millions of tears. He placed it in my lap, as I began to explore the paper so thin so pretty, I notice words, I began to read, with deep anticipation, the words floated off the page. And my heart skipped a beat. The words were from my favorite bible quote: Jeremiah 29:11, For I know the plans I have for you, Declares the lord, plans to prosper you and not harm you, plans to give you hope and a future, I caught my breath, as I thought, "Sometimes this guy amazed me".

My response was Touché, as was most of our responses, when it came to conceding our flag of "know it all ship." We had come to a place in our friendship, where what needed to be said, had been said and we both agreed that the matter was settled. "Never you mind about that", I totally admired his wit and charm, that man had a way of coming alive right at the exact and precise moments, his skills in the art of words were amazing. Nevertheless, in the depth of my soul I felt so pure and I understood exactly what he was saying, he was a gentleman of his word, he was grateful for his charge and his intent was to never complain just live and let live.

Chapter 8

The Courage

There is a quote which can be found anywhere in this world, which states: Any tree can be known by the fruit it bears and likewise a man by the deeds he will and has sown'

As the book of Matthews 7:16-20 states:

Ye shall know them by their fruits. Do men gather grapes of thorns, or figs of thistles?
17 Even so, every good tree bringeth forth good fruit; but a corrupt tree bringeth forth evil fruit.
18 A good tree cannot bring forth evil fruit, neither can a corrupt tree bring forth good fruit.
19 Every tree that bringeth not forth good fruit is struck down, and cast into the fire.
20 Wherefore, by their fruits ye shall know them.

He wasn't openly boisterous, but he had humor.
He wasn't all shiny and forward, but he had style, charm and grace
He wasn't the life of the party, but he was willing to show up
He wasn't the first to speak, but when he spoke, it drew a thought from the conscience of man.
He wasn't the know it all guy, but he would sit up until 5 am, trying to figure it out, so that wisdom would be his guide
That was Kevin's fruit...those were Kevin's deeds

Your fruit is your character,
your fruit is your response,
your fruit is your ability to perform task without selfish
motives, recognition or a pat on the back,
your fruit is your love, drive, compassion and willingness
to press on in spite of the hell, high waters, death,
destruction or doors that close when you are only trying to
do what is right.
Your fruit is knowing full well there are those who say,
they are with you from the hitch to the bumper, and yet
those are the very same ones who place daggers in your
back.

Kevin possessed great fruits,, i watched him smile and
keep it moving, even in the face of great struggles, because
his character was built on a fruit unfamiliar to most,
because he preferred using effort as a fruit of resolution, in
matters of the heart, of the people and of their needs.

His courage surpassed any type of prideful spirit he had,
as showed with his volunteer spirit, such as the many times
he donated his time to the Services of the Community. He
served at the senior center very often, helping deliver food
door to door or making plates to pass out as seniors arrived.
He invited me to participate, to collect donations, some
others liked taking pictures to post on face book, as a way
of showing off their charitable service, but not him, he
hated the pictures that were taken, he thought certain
services were to be kept private, he preferred secrecy, he
said all people deserved privacy and the right for humanity
to bless them without the world looking.

I then thought, was it really charity, if you gave bread and posted on a billboard the names of those that you fed. Again, I reasoned in my heart, and out loud, Well Kevin you are right, Jesus and his disciples fed hundreds of thousands, but not one time did he mention a name or take a picture, even the kid with the fish and loaves, was simply called "The Boy". He laughed loudly, the couple at the table next to us looked at him strongly, as if to say, why are you so happy? I quietly whispered, that I could tell they had recently finished sucking down a spoon full of Bitrex and washing it down with prune juice. He said bitrex,? i told him of the time i read a story about bitter substance and bitrex was described as the bitterest substance in the world, He laughed again.

I loved his laughter, the squint around his eyes, even his eyes went from grey to shiny blue when he laughed. Well, that couple eventually went back to minding their own business, but that is how a small town with nosey unhappy people act. On the other hand, trust, me, it isn't all bad because I can recall as a child, the busy bodies are who kept the town safe, we did not need police patrolling, sneakily slithering along back alleys and parking in the dark. In my neighborhood, we had the late-night riders, and early morning investigators, lol well that's what I will call them, they rode around town and kept the law with their piercing hard gazes as they rode pass the teenage hot spot.

Which was known as Pap's Place, The Sunset or the world famous Two Spot aka Demos, Q's and Sammy and Nodra's. Green Lantern, Blue Goose, never to leave out Mrs. Eddy Mae's and those sizzling burgers. The most unbeknownst thing I can't yet comprehend, is how did they get to the parents of the young girls, who were what they call in the wrong places. If they road through and they saw you talking with, standing near, or you looked to happy, in less than 10 minutes your mom, dad, grandparent, aunts or uncle was on the scene. I still can't get how they got the message sent that quickly, it's not like they had cell phones in their cars. Or did they? was there a secret society of parent's club who passed out cell phone, long before we knew they were invented, as a method of keeping the town safe...

I leaned in and whispered those very same words, which in turn brought out another burst of bold loud laughter yet again, and this time that couple looked at us as if we were ruining their one fish sandwich, that they graciously were sharing. Although I wanted to say something slick out my mouth, I knew I was sitting with the Mayor and could not tell them where to get off, so I quietly said how unimpressed they seemed to be with our happiness, wonder what they would think if I broke out in song? So, we packed up our fun, laughter and jokes and strolled down by the Mill Pond Pavilion where we were sure, the fish would not object to our laughter.

He walked into my job, face all red, flushed and sweaty, in the back of my mind I was thinking, dang it, "what now ". He walked over sat in a chair and breathed loudly (that was my sign he wanted attention), I asked slowly, are you ok? What happened now? he said there is this lady with a 700-dollar water bill and she only had a once a month check for 750, some pipes broke underneath her house and this is the result and she's in need. I tried to reach out to the powers that be, but they aren't interested in helping her.

48

They actually want this lady to foot that bill. He then went on to say, he did not want to over step the process, his thing was as Mayor he could possibly out rank them all and force the matter, but in cases like this, he was willing to allow the others to be their own brothers keepers.

Chapter 9

The Lonely

Being caught up in the time when all the underhanded actions of a city and its former keepers of the Gate, were coming to the surface, took extreme planning and maneuvering, which did not leave much time for he and I, neither to go places or to do things, we had to time ourselves, steal away for quick beach walks, conversations, dinners, movies, mall trips, in and out, no lingering. Which became so frustrating for both he and i. In truth, we had determined this to be the best course of action, seeing that he had begun to open several cans of worms and someone had to keep them from getting away, just like crabs that had fallen out of a trap, they all began to scatter, and those who knew the secrets of the crabs, were determined not to see their friends, families and foes be captured.

I had become use to the apology by then, those apologies that came after each failed attempt to get away and relax, if it wasn't one thing it was another, but truly it wasn't a problem for me. I totally understood, running a City was like running a home, as soon as you fix the steps, someone is screaming about the busted pipes, as soon as they were fixed, someone is screaming about the empty refrigerator. So there you have it, I told him to stop apologizing for life and live in it, to be honest an hour here and a couple hours there was ok for me, it gave me the time I needed to stay focus on my life, because most of our time was spend consoling him and the hardships he faced being the new keeper of the gate, and the hateful people who deliberately stood in his face, daring to destroy him simply because he wasn't like them , how dare he actually care about those people, he should only honor us , because we are new, because we've been here forever, we are special, or we only came here to teach you peasant how to live and act, what a joke.

I think apart of his constant apology, with not having a lot of free time, was the fact that he had faced strong adversities in his former friendships and relationships, I think in his heart he was thinking, here I go again, this one will leave also, she will get tired of me, grow lonely and walk away, but what he hadn't learned was that my need was as strong as his, he was my friend, he listened to my agonies and heart breaks, he held my hand when I cried about things, he sat with me when loved ones left this earth, he sought the approval of my children and did his very best to be present in all they did, So, no I would not grow tired of a friend like that, maybe what I was looking for, wasn't grounded in a physical relationship or a devoted puppy, but more in the knowledge that on the days I needed him, he was there.

I oftentimes had to remind him of that very same fact, he then would smile, hug me and say thank you. And I in turn would say, No thank you, you have given me my Woman Back, the first time I said this he asked me what does that mean? I said, let no one fool you this person you see, was not always there, the person who openly invited you into her life, was fighting really hard to keep you out, but with gentleness and kindness you plowed your way pass my Fort Knox barricades along with my boss, who absolutely encouraged me to stop being mean and enjoy life. He would say, don't be like my former employer, open up your heart let someone in, it doesn't have to hurt, you just never know, what you might find, I would say they all are looking for the same thing and I'm not doing that, my boss would say, not all of us guys are like that, just relax and enjoy life, don't waste away and he was right, that Ex-Boss of mine, he was so right.

Let's not think that was the end of the lonely, after convincing him I wasn't leaving, then here comes the people, he loved people, he wanted them to love him. I knew people was hateful and they deliberately sought to destroy him, because they could not bend him to their will, they hated his independence and ability to have an intelligent opinion. They wanted him to be a puppet, they would invite him to dinner and in meeting just to use the opportunity to turn his head and upon determining he was unbreakable, they then turned their hatred on him and sought to kill his spirit and stand in the way of any progress he sought to bring to the city.

They went as far as to openly defy his efforts to move our city out of debt and allow us to be independent, prideful and more modern. Not that his efforts were fruitless, but the fact that he could do it and they were not the leaders of the pack. Someone had allowed all the street dogs to roam free and wreak havoc on the city and now, how dare the dog catcher try an Rhein them in, he's a trouble maker, he's a

Johnny come lately, he's an outsider, he's not even from here and the funny thing was neither was ninety percent of any of us, the gall of those loose lip fools, the kind that oftentimes caused ships to sink, because they drove ships without compasses, directions or a solid plan.

Those were the days his countenance froze, his shiny (do gooder) light would leave his beautiful eyes, which made me sad and mad. Those were the days my fury stood firm, you selfish self-centered fools, how do you dare to reject help, when most of you have no clue whether to turn right or left, most of you are Facebook bully's and front porch complained, if this guys was a Johnny come lately or an outsider, why hadn't none of you generational insiders stepped up and at least tried to help, yes tried to help, (no I did not say get in and turn into the ones who were the oppressors), I said get in set a standard and at least set an effort or standard of sincerity of value, why was the one who wanted to help being victimized or persecuted ? For having a back bone, the audacity to say no more, let's do better, let's set goals, that are attainable and follow through, because of our generational pride and love for the community and its people.

So yes, each time he was rejected it took me days even weeks to talk him down off his, how can I do better? Why don't they like me? What can I do to get folks on board? Why are they rejecting ideas that could bring in progressive progress? Why do they not help me set the atmosphere? I thought they would enjoy the betterment for their community? And there I stood, mad at him for butt kissing and sad for him for wanting better for folks, who didn't give a hill of beans what progress he made, as long as they could play King and Queen of a stolen atmosphere. Lords of the Land and Davey Crocket Owner of the local coastline frontier.

Each time he returned from a party, home visit, boat ride, secret luncheon, back room brawl and email dart throwing. You could see the light sink deeper from his belief in people, that sometimes scared me, because it had been a long time since I 'd witnessed, someone stand up and count the City as a city, not in sections but as a whole City, deep inside me I was thinking,, if he stop caring they are up shit creek, because no one had placed this much effort or actually asked them their opinion and immediately brought it to the city, in search of a solution. This man did and each time he could not pull a rabbit out of a hat, they said he was no good, never mind all the good he had accomplished, for every step he took forward, some self-serving ungrateful idiot would not even count the win, they would automatically say, "well he said he would fix it". As if they were used to the gate keepers doing perfect things, since the beginning of time, "Oh you forgetful, entitled, home grown people".

I actually looked at some of the complainers and could not believe the tenacity it took to say; what he should have done, when those very same folks sat around and watch the fabric of the community die, right before their very eyes, now all of a sudden the burden had fallen on one man's shoulders, and all eyes was on him, to magically remove all

of the wrongs, those "know it all naggers" could have had
done, long before he ever entered the town, had they
stepped up years before. Instead, they now are making one
man feel as if it was all his fault, walking pass him refusing
to speak or acknowledge his presence, because their water
bill went up three dollars, when it wasn't his doing, that
sent it in that directions in the first place.

Where were all the watchers at then? how did it get so
out of hand? And why was this man being demonized for
something that happened years, (decades even) before his
ascend? My city loves scapegoats, he was prime meat for
the goat herders, who was gunning to find someone to set
on that pedestal. And he was a prime target simply because
he wore his heart on his sleeve, and wanted to change the
world, and if not the world, but the city he lived in, the city
he had passion for, the city he thought was worth delivering
from their own perils of afflictions and doom determined
by their own hands, caught in a web of lies and eye closure
attitudes, set to not give two hoots as to what was
happening right in front of their faces, but now all of a
sudden everyone is singing, I can see clearly now, because
they have found someone to blame or cast their lots upon.

I think I will feel the loneliest on the days there is no
one there to lean in and pass me nuggets of knowledge:

He would lean in close to my mouth as if he was going
to kiss me and say;

Zebra have stripes that are unique on their forehead and
the mother zebra takes the baby away for a while after its

55

birth, so that the baby zebra will become connected personally to the mom

No one knows when she will return, with that baby,

they need time to bond. The middle stripes in the zebra forehead is unique like human's finger prints.

For example orange wine mixed with any flavor can transcend a particular flavor or brand into a scientific wonder or something elegant like, when he said that Sam Cooke made him dream of me, Oh yeah the Bee Gees held a place in his heart also, because they were brothers and they had a bond, Kevin cherished bonds, he would sometimes add that there is nothing better than likeminded people working together to accomplish a single goal.. it is more satisfying than an orgasm... and better than winning the lottery. "Yeah, he had jokes", he threw shade and he was quick on the draw, I often would look at folks after they thought they had gotten one over on him and thought "just you wait, he'll be back and when he does." There will be hell to pay...

Sometimes the pain of what he missed overtook him, the thought of having his own children, raising his own sons and cherishing his own daughters, those were some of the heart wrenching do overs he desired   There was a kid who lived across the street from him (Colton), A very curious and lovely boy, one who could hold a conversation as if he was an adult, this child made an everlasting expression on Kevin, while he and I were sitting on his porch one night or late evening, the boy walked out his door waved at us picked up an item from his yard and went back in the house. Kevin smiled and said, if I had been given the chance to have a kid I bet he would have been brilliant just like that kid and point across the street. Months later, maybe about a couple weeks before Kevin passed, i had the opportunity to share this story with the kid's mom. She was grateful for the love Kevin gave her sons. She said his presence made a difference in their lives as a neighbor and as a person to look up too.

Kevin would have been a great father, I watched him near my children and on a few occasions with my grands, especially Nyah, he thought she was so intelligent, he said Nyah would not easily be swayed on any level. He said she had inherited my gumption and verbal capacity, in other words she talked smack and wasn't going to put up with people stuff lol.. he described her as being a dark chocolate beauty, he said he had seen her look on many foreign black children, it was an earthly exotic feature. He said she would use it one day to heal a nation or control it. She would and could decide. Again in other words her beauty would serve her well.

He described Trinity as being the perfect daughter, he said any man would be proud of her, this was during the time of her engagement, he had begun to feel a little sick or tired in his body and he wanted me to make sure her wedding went well (he definitely made sure that happened). He said those were the things he missed about not having a daughter, someone to walk down an aisle. He had decided it would have been cruel, to bring kids into this world with his taste for adventure and travel, but on days like this, melancholy took over and regret did set in. He smiled and said well I guess I'll tag along with you and enjoy my part.

All isn't lost, usually all isn't lost was his way of hiding behind his disappointment, pain, grief, regret and loss.

I was so glad he had a friend, Tommy Ward (of 13-Mile Seafood, with 2 locations), was Kevin's friend. Kevin raved on and on about Tommy, Patty and the children and how grateful he was for their friendship, love and welcoming spirit. He talked about having a hiding place from the hurricane and any other needed situation. He loved the Ward family, someone once made mention to me about him hanging out with the wealthy, and I quickly dismissed that theory, I had listened to Kevin and his only attraction to those people, were the fact that they were kind, money or prestige had no place in Kevin's desired love and respect toward them.

He had a certain type of atmosphere and a certain reason for his attentiveness, for example he loved it when he and I went to Dockside Restaurant, he said he enjoyed watching me blush, under the gumptions of restaurant owner Trey. As well as his having a fondness for the Apalachicola Grill, he told me once that Mrs. Beverly, who is one of the owners, had the most beautiful smile and was very peaceful to be near. He said she made eating there enticing. He also said, if I was ever in need of great chicken salad or homemade cakes, Delores Sweet Shop was the place to go. I knew all these things, I could not tell him that, I would sit there and enjoy how he enjoyed this little paradise called Apalachicola and the many attractions.

It wasn't until the loneliness of the Sunshine Law kicked in, that he felt off beat, with the rule of the sunshine law and his position of mayor, made for a tight lipped situation, whereas before his ascend, he could share whatever came to mind or pressed his heart, but after his oath, be had so much on his mind, but could not dare share it with me, that would have been against the law, and Kevin was never one to bend the law, not even for person release. So, I oftentimes suggested he get a therapist. Because there were things, simple things, but important things he would need to leave at the feet of someone who had the position to carry those things. I did my best, but I too knew there was a line that could not be crossed, but secretly, I did not want to know about all the foolishness of that part of it.

Chapter 10

The Secrets

Today was his birthday, he had a thing about his birthday, he said he never wanted anyone to make a fuss, he wanted it kept as a secret. But in my heart, I knew that was a lie, he did want a fuss, he did want a party, he did want gifts, what he did not want really, was to be a bother too folks, he did not want to ask folks for things, he wanted them to offer out of their desires to be kind, how do I know this? because each year for the pass three, when I gave him gifts and surprised him he would just smile and say the same thing each year, how did you know it was my birthday, that was his way of being happy without looking overly excited, I could tell he wasn't the kind who was given things often.

I had gathered that people were so familiar with taking from him, no one ever stopped to see if he needed something. And it came to fruition at that point, so I just never mentioned it again, I just made plans and saw them through, he enjoyed it, the look on his face each time was priceless, although I'm sure he knew it was coming, he did not know what, but he had grown to know me enough to know, I would never let his birthday pass without honoring him on his day. I did cherish the look on his face, when I gave him gifts and surprised him he would just smile, he would stand there like a goofy kid grinning and happily accepting whatever he was given, he was a thankful person, because no matter what he got he would use it, I would see him putting it to use.

He had a lot of notions in that manner, for example, when he won the election he assumed those who urged him to run, those of his campaign party and those so gun ho at his changing our community, would have given him a victory celebration, Well that did not happen and he expressed his sadness about that, so what did I do? I got together with some of my friends and coworkers we took him out. Although those in my party had not actually been on team Begos, they were my friends and they honored him non the less. You should have seen the sparkle in his eye, he was very humble and quite joyed to know, that someone cared enough to show him off as Mayor.

Those were some of the things that he and I held as secrets, just a fragment of the many things which plagued his heart, he wanted to be liked, he never wanted to disappoint, he sometimes would shut down his opinion, if it would satisfy the masses. He sometimes would agree to things just to keep the peace. He believed in following peace with all men, he never wanted to look like the aggressor and I think, those were the times I had double emotions towards him, first sympathy for his plight as Mayor and a Human and frustration for him as a Man, I just could not grasp his heart strings, how he would let folks pull on them to the point, that it took the glimmer out of his beautiful eyes.

61

But, in hindsight those were the qualities which drew me to him in the first place, His quiet strength, there is a saying "may the life I lead speak for me, may the work I've done speak for me". That was his secret motto, he never wanted to openly brag or say woe it was me, He simply hoped that he had done a good enough job, which would prick the hearts of man and they would show kindness. I think above all, above millions of dollars and statues of gold, he craved kindness. I recall sitting at a dinner table with him and several of our companions, they began to ask him question, questions that required his opinion and expertise, his face lit up like a Christmas tree, he was in his element.

He was shy, he couldn't openly talk about romance, sex, relationships, dating, or any of the stuff that normal guys got together and discussed, or who could pee the farthest, but if you put him in front of a group talking about humanity and the plight of man, he would steal the show. So, I sat there watching him control the room, it made my heart happy to see him, come out of his shell, this shell was hard to penetrate, he was more of an action guy not really a word guy, especially if it came from his lips. I know some would disagree, because they only saw him in his work capacity, they only saw him on the campaign trail, or in pursuit to righting some wrongs, that had occurred to his constituents, especially those things he had campaigned on.

(Well except for this one time, he called me and said well I'm sure you will find out, so I better clear it up now, I was with Jeff Lockley and we ran into his friend George Davis aka Buddy Love, he was going on and on about finding girls, so I chimed in and told him to find one for me also, Now I am really not looking for one and you know this, but I was with the guys and I had to say something to fit in, "I actually pretended like I was jealous", but deep inside my soul I was so proud of him, he was hanging with the fellas and he made guy jokes. Wow what an impressive feat for someone like Kevin, who would never or rarely indulge in maleness. I just wanted to find Buddy and Jeff and hug them.}

There was no way on this side of earth he would ever back down, from what he had promised people he would do, whether he had to slide in through the back door, or on top of the roof, he was coming in and doing just what he said he would. One more reason to trust him, he kept his word, words were bond with him, life and memory of the reasons and situations he had overcome was another, he believed that those whom had been blessed to see a better life, get another chance, live free, live long, live in peace and still remember the former things, should with all their hearts bring that very same energy to the table, so that others would have the chance to eat from the fat of the land.

It absolutely broke his heart when he thought of rejection, folks turning their backs on one another, especially those folks who by the skin of their teeth and because of some opportune point, were also blessed and given more than they dared dream of. His soul could not comprehend the tenacity it took to treat people unfairly, I often looked at him silently and wondered how someone with the depth of intellect he possessed, could be so gullible, he was quiet gullible when it came to people, that was the one thing he had not mastered, he mastered politics, he mastered reparations, he mastered exposure to crimes against man and woman, he mastered peace with other countries, he mastered finding peace in his soul for the wrongs he had committed and those committed unto him, he also mastered degrees in college, but not one time could he master man's heart.

That oftentimes would break his heart, he was the kid in the candy store who wanted everybody to have some, he was the kid who brought all the other kids to his mother's front door, so that when his mom gave him a snack, she would be obligated to feed the other kids also. Secrets are a powerful thing, some we wear on our sleeve for the world to analyze, even if they aren't sure what they see and some are embedded in the hearts of man, those are the ones that late night conversations are made of, those are the ones that are not exactly the dinner table type talks, those are the kind which takes patience, love and strength to reveal.

I did not instantly know I was on trial, but maybe about a year into our friendship be boldly made a statement, although this statement would have shocked a lot of people, me personally my skin was tougher than some frilly silly girl, I had long since realized that we all are humans and we all have places on our road of life ,that we weren't always on the straight and narrow. Well as straight and narrow as some folks made it out to be. Although the words pierced my inner being, I kept it cool, I continued eating, "mostly because something inside of me said he's testing your endurance and he's testing your strength and friendship…

He then said did you hear me, I smiled and said; yes, I heard you!!! Isn't this food good, thank you for introducing me to this cuisine and then I said is that all you got? I then took a crowbar plied open the door to my skeleton closet and museum, I then began to share a few things with him. He smiled nodded his head and tipped his cup, the smile almost burst through his skin, as I thought, no sir Mr. Mayor, you cannot offend or shock me with simple things such as that, you gotta step up your game brother, if you intend to pierce me or want me to squirm, "poor guy"(he had no idea, I spent most of my years around three strong willed women, Mama, Mary and Margie) and these women left no stone unturned.

At that moment our window opened, and we knew life goes on and so should we. Although that was not the end of things, because there will always be what life calls haters, they definitely wanted him to know I had a pass and to bring his to my face, we both would lick our wounds and retreat back to each other and report the outside comments, I have looked in the face of what are suppose to be friends, but are really foes, not even until today, do they know, that I know, that they were culprits in the scheme to destroy our friendship, not because we had invented the cure for cancer, or that we were some overly happy couple, not even

65

that we shined as we walked down the street, it was simply because we had a friendship and we were not taking membership applications.

We were us and that was that, no conversation, no explanation, no public displays, no invitation, just us, friends with a built-in soul tie. We had no idea when it began or how long it would last, but we both knew sitting at that table eating Thai Cuisine, that nothing we said to each other or anyone else said about each other, would ever sever our friendship. I think silently in our hearts we knew, we had found that simple single person who would not judge or look down against our lives or use our pass indiscretions, as a Scarlett Letter or a way to count our abilities to perform as decent human being. With souls sent to add flavor to this already bland existence we call human life.

He revealed to me, that someone once proposed marriage to him, he did not have the nerves or balls to say no, so he let it ride, almost up until the wedding day, I never asked her name, that would have been to much information, That was one of those things that bothered him, he wished he had the strength to say no not now, or I don't feel that way about you or maybe lets wait until we know each other better, but instead he just walked in an unwanted engagement. His heart felt bad, he so wanted to call that person up and say he was sorry and that he was absolutely afraid to commit, because he had witnessed so much unfairness in marriages, he had personally lived in the front row seat of tragedy in marriages and relationships,

He was stone cold afraid to give all he had and be tossed by the wayside again.

If you looked closely in his eyes, when he talked about such things, you could actually see his fear, which gave me chills, he was afraid of commitment and I was angry about commitments. Two peas in a pod of opposite truths. What a pair of deer caught in the headlights of life, one to scared to commit and the other one vowing never to do so again, because she (me) knew love held a do not enter sign. So, we sat there eating our food whilst planning in our heads, how to hold on to our friendship without passing on our demons, without shifting the other to a place where that person would become frightened and run. Because we both knew, in the middle of all our politeness, manners, grace, intellect, we were both still frightened flawed humans without a map to the future.

About a week after that conversation, he hit me with another secret, the one where he tells me how long he had noticed me and how difficult I made it for him to approach me, he said; he had noticed me on occasions, as I strolled into a local bar/restaurant called Up To No Good, that was the place we frequented usually on Friday nights.(We called it wind down from work outing). We came in as if we were the local celebrities, and within minutes our table would be swamped with food and drinks, in the beginning he said he thought we (Myself, Donna and Penny) were uppity and unapproachable, as time progressed he noticed that I was a hugger and a talker, then he thought, well maybe she isn't that bad after all.

He said; he even spoke to me once and when I spoke back, it was with a gigantic smile, he went on to tell me how my smile felt so warm and real, from that moment on, he knew he wanted to know why I smiled so deeply and did that smile have room for him. (I told you he was a charmer), he spoke of how he made it his business to seek me out, with each passing opportunity and every time he became ready to say something, I would frighten him away, because my conversation with others, my tone, my exactness, my boldness, my no holds punching, my sarcastic undertones, spoke volumes. His thought was that I would not be willing to undertake a simple fellow such as himself, in other words I looked like a hand full, with legions of suiters and a overly determined spirit.

Eventually, at the grocery store, he threw caution to the wind and decided to offer me pasta, he was hoping he picked right, and I then told him how frightened he made me, how could some stranger know which pasta I liked and yes I knew he was there, I even told my boss and co-worker I had a stalker, and not to mention he was everywhere, all over the place, now that I think about it, he was there at the restaurant always eating pizza and drinking non- alcohol beer. But everyone there ate pizza and beer, and yes, I had tunnel vision, my motto was to go in, sit down, order my food, tend to my business, maybe the people with the wondering drunk hands would slide pass me and seek out some other person to attack. But most times that never happened, they liked me, I liked them, so usually some guy would make a pass, but who cared, I would smile and keep it moving, we knew what would happen, so we kept to ourselves most of the time.

Perhaps that is why he saw me as standoffish or maybe he was right, I can be downright unapproachable at times, I often do have a plan in my head, I'm not interested, I don't have time to play games, and most of the usable ones are married and married wasn't my cup of tea, so I strolled in, sat down and played catch up with my friends Donna and Penny. We mostly were so engrossed in our own stories and life changing events. There really was no time for anyone else, either we would be laughing, crying or pledging loyalty to our bitter man hating lives or man bashing team, we were one hundred percent determined we had all the answers and we hated, just hated when someone would come up to our table, well unless they were paying our tab.

He had an idea to buy the Bar called Qs and refurbish all the sides. He said he did not want to see the Hill area evaporate and if it fell in the wrong hands, the only living black owned business would be gone. so, he and I went to have a meeting with the owner and her niece. Also, he went to discuss it with the bank. Finally, we ended up back at his house. I often drove when we went out on business, that gave him time to plot his plan, he said we needed to talk, I turned the car off and looked him straight on. he said Rose you do realized I'm getting old and I wasn't blessed to have kids of my own, nor does my sister have kids. So, I'm thinking you need to start looking for a name for that place.

Because truthfully this business will be for your kids. you don't need to do anything, you don't need to put any money in it. I got that. I just need you to promise me you will put all your imagination and sass in our business. I sat there, unable to speak, there were no words that would have fixed how I felt at that moment. I could feel tears falling from my eyes, he said please don't cry, of course you knew I had your back right? At that moment, I realized how it felt to have someone love you and your children, enough to want the best for them. Although we did not get it. That wasn't the point. The point was that he wanted something better for us. That was how he loved. He loved in real time. He loved from his soul

He loved this town so much he sacrificed his health. He first stated that he was to do his treatments for his myocarditis, from Panama City to Pensacola. The next thing i knew, he had me contacting someone to get him an ambulance ride back to the local facility here, to be really honest, I had no desire for him to be here with his condition. For me that wasn't what I desired for him. But he was insistent on, "as he put it", if money from insurance was going to be spent, it should go to MY community, still worried about this town. I know God had his plans already set, but if I'm telling the truth, then I had deep reservations. Not about the hospital, but because he required some extensive care,

I felt that he needed a more state of the art facility. But those were the things he wanted to change, he wanted to prove that we could do better, and by doing so he would stand in the gap, use his heart, mind, soul and body to

70

prove that our town, our doctors, our hospitals, our restaurants, our kindness, our love, our respect was worth fighting for, yes he knew other facilities had more intense care, but he wanted to prove to the world that our town could do and be better. Even to the very end, he placed his trust in the underdog, he opened up his soul to change the indifference we faced in our community.

He had this hardcore fascination with draw bridges, he was soon to write a piece on them, women workers of the bridges, two women in particular Bonnie Russ Jones and Carrie Ratliff, Jones tended historical Apalachicola's John Gorrie Bridge and Ratliff tended old Siesta Key Bridge in Sarasota. I guess I probably could produce the piece with my eyes closed, seeing that he wore my ear off, with (details) about those thing's so often. (But that's not my story to tell it was his). Something about women opening draw bridges was like a mother opening her arms of love, to welcome someone in. All the boats that went out, went out with the blessings of love, enough to help seal their ability to catch a healthy bounty and returning to open arms of welcome, for their ability to provide for their families, friends and community.

I have a funny Secret:
One of his Mayoral projects for the CRA district was redeveloping the 6th Street Parks basketball and tennis courts, this guy made me ride with him pass that place 6 times in 20 minutes, oh my god, he was bursting with pride as he drove up and down, back and forth!!!!! But that was his heart, he was very pleased, his goal was to see people

71

happy and to refurbish their usable environment, somehow
it told him, somewhere inside his loving heart, that people
wanted prideful environments to look upon and cherish.
(now let me just say this, I thought 6 times was over kill,
but I never said a word, I smiled and said Bravo Kevin you
have done
well)

Chapter 11

(Debate) Philosophical and Theological

He invited me to his house, I asked for his address, he would not give it to me, he smiled and said figure it out. At first, I was like this guy is playing games, but later I learned, that was his way of thinking if a person had real interest, they would find out what they needed to know. That investigation and journalistic side of him never stop turning.

Kevin's gifts were shown in its brightest form, as he delved into his philosophical knowledge and mine in my theological knowledge. Which sometimes made for very Heated and Humorous debates. Somewhere around the third month of our friendship, I recall saying something along the lines of, well Kevin, I am sorry If all of my answers revolve around a scripture, he then looked me square in the face and said; never stop talking about your God, I never said i didn't believe in God, I just sometimes find it difficult to believe in people. He truly did love people,, their food, cultures, accents, knowledge, peace and humor, he sometimes found it difficult to comprehend the heart of man though.

He then proceeded to describe Kevin the 12 yr. old boy, who was healed from cancer and Kevin the baby who was born prematurely, in Marseilles France,, while his parents (Jane and Kevin Sr) proudly served our country as Military leaders. He described those events and other periods in his life with glee, as if they were his badge of honor, in other words, regardless to whether he discussed it or not, whether he stood in a room full of folks and quoted scriptures or not, he was still a believer in God, and that he still trusted him in his comings and goings. He smiled and described France, his parents, his sister, he talked about his travels and he made sure I understood that there was no line separating him and god, he just had his own way of serving him, and I respected that.

He was right, I was right, his point was true and mine was too. That's how it went, one day we were up, one day we were down. Depended on who scored the most points, no I'm not talking about ball, cards or chess, I'm talking about debate, debate, debate!!!! That's how we had fun, we debated. His love for Philosophical thinking and mine of the Theological persuasion. Neither idea stopped the debates though, both he and I gave strongly as we got, he and I believed in our opinions and we stuck to our guns, I learned a lot in those discussions, my knowledge box became filled each time we went for the top prize of who was right. I can truly say he pricked my spirit and opened doors to deeper thinking, which taught me that my determination and dedication to always be right or have the last word wasn't always necessary.

You never knew which Kevin you were going to meet, His taste for the joys of the world varied, I had come to know when he had another part of himself to show me, he would smile and say there is something you need to see, He then would usually leave the room to retrieve his "whatever". On one occasion, he returned holding something, it was a small album of photos, from his days of being in a boy band. He never would guide me in any of his shares, he would always hand me the object and let me examine it or discover what lied beneath for myself. His taste in music was another extreme matter, His personality changed with his music, there were times I walked into his home and Tibetan singing bowl and flute music would meet me at the door. Then there were times Percy Sledge would seep through the walls singing ("when a man loves a woman" ...) Kevin's had a beautiful singing voice, I guess he learned that being the lead singer of a rock band called "The Twilights".

Unless you were close enough to him, that one fact would never show its face. And show it face it did, sometimes after a couple drinks of wine, the loose lip Kevin would sing songs, on those occasions the true Kevin honored me with his presence, not the face of the mayor, politician, constituent or someone he needed to present a perfect face in front of. He honored me with the man who could and would cry, the man who had shame, the man who had fears and tears, the man who wasn't always sure, the man who didn't always watch what he said, nor cared about being right, nor being dressed up or smiling.

He gave me the real him, he gave me secrets to help him carry, or wounds that needed prayer. He gave me a shoulder to lean on and a friend that stood taller than the statue of liberty. heart as a gentleman, brother, son, lover, neighbor, friend, homeowner, flower planted, fruit grower and connoisseur of fine wine, women, travel and food. This may sound like some billionaire sowing wild oats and being adventurous, but on the contrary, these were the vices used to keep him focused. So, I honor him in all the places he planted his feet, in all the lives he touched, in all the gardens on earth and in hearts he has sown a seed or touched.

Things weren't always holding hands and singing in the rain, we both were petty and picky, sometimes down right cruel. For example the day I discovered he had a fear of wedding, I would catch him right when he was getting ready to relax and I would show him a picture of a wedding dress and say isn't that beautiful, of course he would say yes or that it had too much lace and sometimes he would just look at me, I had known how to put on my serious face, during my times of mental Russian Roulette, the fear that overtook him was so funny at times, I almost would burst into laughter, but it was a game and we both played it well, it was how we kept each other on our toes.

I often attended weddings or performed ceremonies, and each time I did, I usually would catch the bouquet and it would frighten Kevin so much, he would call me constantly for days afterward inquiring about "my marital state of mind", he was so frightened that I was going to bring up marriage, he tip toed around me, I guess he was thinking the fever would hit me, and what he truly did not know was I had no thoughts on it period, but it was to funny to pass up, I did not have enough nicety to admit it, I just let him squirm, I knew I should have not turned the knife so deep, but he was just as vicious as me, there were times he pulled some hardcore scams on me as well.

He would smile or blow wind through his tightly gripped lips, which he often did, when he really wanted to say something crazy, but chose not to. Those were the times he would have taken special thought, of a way to push me to my uncomfortable place. Especially during the times, he would go out on business luncheons with women, He would call, text or drop by, just to say he hope I didn't mind but he was out with so and so, or he would say something like; so and so asked me to lunch what do you think, should I go? And normally I would say go, because eventually I knew from the smirk in his eyes, he was flat out going for the jugular, and I dared not bite the bullet.

We absolutely one hundred percent knew exactly which buttons to push, which words to say, which expressions to make, which part of a conversation to cut short, and which smile to perpetrate, which made for interesting games. I'm sure a lot of it was for fun and I definitely knew a lot of it was for skill, his skill or mine, the fittest of the fittest, the keen of the keen, the joyous of the joyous. We were determined not to falter at the hand of the other, we were determined to exercise our right to power, not any harmful kind, but power none the less, the kind that would serve us well in the coming months.

One particular debate comes to mind, the one where he and I read about Adam and what was said to be his first wife Lilith, the story went on to talk about their debate over sexual positions, that they each was created with both sexual organs and one day Lilith decided it was her turn to be on top, we laughed as we read this, you can imagine how deep this made our conversation, with massive ifs, and or buts. I reasoned as a twenty first century woman, that indeed Lilith desired to be on top but not sexually, she wanted her opinion to count, she wanted to be recognized as an equal partner, she wasn't so desperate for recognition as she was to be seen and respected in who she was and what she brought to the table also,

I thought of this passage of word as a parable to life, as we sometimes forget to understand other people needs. He then delved into the fact that scientifically it was possible that they both were born in that manner, seeing that others have been. And it was just as well possible, once Lilith discovered all things work together, she wanted her turn on top, as would be a reasonable request (i stated). He then stated that early man has always been man, conceived with the concept of superiority, and would never have allowed for this, and I being flippant in my approach said, well I guess the new age man has changed his mind. We both laughed and kept on in our divulging of out of space thoughts.

This conversation lasted for 4 hours, we talked, laughed, made up imaginary stories and yet until today, I can only imagine this as a cry from women all around the world to be heard and not just seen and used. At the end of our parched mouth and dry throat conversation, he said do you as a Christian believe she was real? I sat up because the law between Christianity and Philosophy had a doubled edged sword. I was not about to dare answer that question head on. I knew he would crush me, so i said, I believe in any concept that allows gods children to be heard and treated fairly. He laughed and said; "good answer" the cameras would have loved that one. But then I went on to say, what

78

about Adam and his superiority or male ego and masculine need to be on top, can you see that as a truth in men. He said I'm hungry let's eat. So, we laughed.

Our friendship could never be described nor received as therapy, but there was a therapeutic element to this friendship. We both believed in Frivolous Entertainment, he personally thought those events opened the mind and relaxed our souls, which gave way to peace and creativity. For example, I had a deck of cards which ask questions, he saw them sitting on a table next to my bed. He inquired into what they were? and I explained that sometimes when I was alone, while the house was quiet. I would shuffle them, read the question and answer truthfully, honestly and without reservation.

He liked that idea, eventually that game became a part of our friendship. He would say are you coming over today, bring the cards, let's do truth. Or when he showed up at my house and he needed to be real, he would say ask me a question, that meant it was card time. Believe it or not I found out a lot about that man through our frivolous entertaining times and he in return found out some of the hidden secrets about me, things I swore were only meant for God and the grave. But my dear friend Kevin found his way beneath the surface and into my truth and my card game.

Sometimes we took it to far, sometimes our games caused each other pain, I won't lie, we both played who

79

could flinch and we did it with deliberate intent. I call it who could flinch, because we would say things to one another just to see who would flinch or become overly bothered.

We loved our friendship and regardless to how we both protest, we wanted the other to prove love, so we would say or do things that would bring out the jealousy, just to keep the other on their toes. He usually came full throttle all at once, but not me, nope not always, I was a tad bit more manipulating, and as a woman, I took time to simmer in my retaliation. So, he just never knew when, where or what was coming or how.

Like I said, some of our antics were downright cruel, as I think about it, perhaps we both knew that was our foreplay way. We wanted each other sharp, thinking and watchful at all times. We knew that if we couldn't handle each other's shenanigans, someone else's games would swallow us whole. For that reason alone, we weren't about to let that happen. Not that we both had not gone through times, when the hound dogs came out, presenting themselves as innocent puppies, but we both saw straight through them. We would eventually retreat and inform the other, with a laugh and watchful eye.

I must admit, there were times when it looked as if our enemies would win, but being of level headed, common sense friends we prevailed. We ignored the voices that loomed in the dark, trying to destroy our peace and friendship. I often would look the enemy right in their faces thinking, you underhanded dog, do you not know that I know, who you are. In that arena Kevin took top prize,

because he would not stew in it, when it came near him, he
would manipulate the situation by using his Journalist
skills, he probed them for vital information(whether it was
true or not) just to see how far he could get them to go.

Yep we lived for the love of the games, whether it was
us taunting each other or whether it was other's actually
thinking they were taunting us..
However we were very good opponents and at the end of
the day or end of the game, we both would return to our
special space in each other, as victors and with usable
information. Yep, some would call that friends who had the
other's back. Sometimes to others, it may have looked like
the opposite, but no, it was all a part of knowing the game
and willing to stay the course for the sake of self and what
we had determined to be worth the cause.

While reading a passage from his book Against Their
Will, he posed a question to my theologian mind, he said if
more than 7600 sterilizations occurred during a 49 year
span and no one asked your God or got his permission to
kill those babies, who do you think he will hold
responsible, for the murder of all the unborn children?
doctors, lawyers teacher, preacher, garbage worker, cooks,
Olympic team mates, sailors and politicians? Who? Well,
you know me, I immediately jumped on board that
question. With the phrase "all of them" everyone who
participated, all of them who approved it being done, all
who sat around knowing it was being done and did not do a
thing to stop it. Because the Bible says we should bare the
infirmities of the weak, whether that be the babies or their
disabled, young, unaware, uneducated, poverty stricken and
uninformed mothers.

He kissed my forehead smiled and said, well I guess my

hands are clean, I wrote about it, which led to reparations, but I can't take all the credit, me and my team did it. He loved that team of people he spoke about the woman with the original concept and how she welcomed him into her home and shared her inner thoughts on all matters concerned, he raved about the research team and the editors. I think Kevin was the proudest of himself for meeting those people and the heart and soul they added to this journey. He said some of his best days in life, were spent righting this wrong and giving the dead and those still alive a peace, a voice. and a respect for their human value.

Saturday August 7th, 2021 is yet another National Lighthouse Day. And Kevin you won't be around to enjoy it. He loved our local lighthouse, he loved all lighthouses. He mentioned that his working at that lighthouse had nothing to do with money, it was all about the adventures he partook in, while meeting strangers, he had so many story's he was privy to, because the visitors loved to share, sometimes on his way up and down those flights of stairs he gained great knowledge, there would be times, by the time he reached the bottom of the stairs he knew people entire family tree, he loved that job, he loved those people, he loved touching lives as they touched his.

He made mention of the former light house keepers and how he wondered if they sat their day after day, night after night alone. He wondered if they had used those alone moments to embrace their sadness and rejoice spiritually in their gladness, he had wondered if they cried over lost moments and disappointment, he wondered if they were loners and wished for togetherness. He said being a lighthouse keeper, one had the opportunity to seek peace. He said sitting high and looking low, sometimes gave you a perspective of just how earthly we really are.

He had full Intent to bring their legacy to life, we sat for hours whilst he tickled my ears, mind and imagination as to their thoughts and prayers while alone and with god. The stories we came up with and the conversations we imagined were amazing. This would have been a great story. He was so incredible, and he helped my impulsiveness to explode when he opened any subject, also giving me full rein at advancing my ripe and deadly grip on the truth, untruth and the how I see it ability. That alone was dangerous, seeing that I had the power to stretch myself way beyond the norm almost to a point of did you really say that? are you really thinking that? Did that actually come out of your mouth and head?

So, as I sit here today, I toast you Mr. Lighthouse Keeper for the time you spend in that tower growing in your wisdom and spirit.

Chapter 12

The Fights

Our main fights always revolved around politics and opponents. I would dig my feet in so deep, at any mention of me and political office. My response would be a resounding hell no never. I would say Kevin they would impeach me in a week, because when one of those wimpy whiny ass people, would step up to that podium and deliberately disrespect me, for some tom foolery, I would curse them out Hard. which I'm sure would give David Adlerstein our Newspaper Man something juicy to write about and Amy Hersey something to record.

Yes, he was sweet and kind, but he also had the I wanna have it my way streak sometimes. Although he did not come right out and say it, he had an undertone of sneaky manipulating power lurking in him.

Oh, wow this fight was worse than the others, our difference of opinion this time, caused a tear in our hope, a tear in our dreams, a tear in our words, a tear in our trust. This discussion took both of us to a place, we should not have gone, but we did. We fought, and this time it was vicious. My anger and hurt could not see pass anything he had to say, his desire to be right pushed him in a corner and he wasn't willing to come out, at this point there was no turning back. we took our aggressions out on one another, we both are verbal people and had found the pressure places in each other, that could trigger defeat. This is what happens when people open their hearts up, while sharing their inner feeling, we give way to parts of us that are usable for controlling the outcome of other people's fears and griefs.

Those are the things that bite you right in the face, while you are not looking, those are the things that sometimes push us pass the point of no return and for a minute we were borderline vicious. Not because we did not love or respect each other, Sometimes the best of friends finds themselves in an awkward position, someone once said iron will rust and PVC pipes can break. I guess that is where we were on that day, in between a rock and a hard place, he needed to be right and so did I, neither of us were willing to bend, maybe because he had bent over backward for the public and I had bent over backwards for him. We both had inner turmoil we hadn't dared to share or speak out loud, so here we stood flat foot, shouting, irritated, stubborn, outright outrageous and dead wrong, both of us.

He was wrong for taking out on me, the anger he had felt for years, from other people, other places, other relationships, other friendships, others trust and other lives. And I was angry because no matter how hard I try to add people to my life, there always seem to be someone who forget to see me, forget to put me first, forget to add my needs to the equation, and forget to put me first. On that day we both had not bothered to see each other, we were both ready to let it all out. Perhaps somewhere deep inside of us, we knew that screaming at each other was ok, or would be ok, maybe we knew that no matter how much we screamed, we could still see deep inside each other and move pass it.

Well that's not how it happened, I stormed out, he stood still, and no one spoke for three weeks, we were right back where we started from three years ago, strangers, passing each other in the store, seeing each other in the park, walking pass each other at meeting, without uttering one single word. While alone, my peace said; call him, apologize, but the stubborn me said, nope let him call you. And that's how it went inside my head for three weeks, on the cusp of the third week, my phone rang at 4;45 pm, he said; Hello, I am hoping that we can talk, can we talk please, Immediately I said yes.

As I walked through his door, that familiar smell of manly clean soap and history, slapped me in the face. He smiled and said. I've missed you and I am sorry, and I was wrong, we sat and discussed why we felt the need to crush each other's dreams, to throw back in each other's faces all the things that haunted us, all the things that took us away from our stability. I'm not at all saying we were in anyways right, but as adults we determined ourselves to be frustrated with other things, that should not have been taken to that extreme and we vowed that we would have disagreements, but we would cover each other hearts not damage them.

He had a meeting once and i swear afterward, I saw this look on his face, as if the life and light had been sucked from his body. By that time, I had learned to just sit there and let him talk, until he found a way to get it out. He would start off diplomatic using all the right verbs and adverbs, putting all the commas in conjunction to his phrases as if he was talking to someone else. Eventually he would come back to himself and realize it was just me, and the true Kevin would surface. He Said Rose, do you know what happened to me today? (that wasn't really a question, it actually was a statement that meant he was about to go deep) it required no answer, I just became attentive to his words, he wanted my attention when he made statements of such.

He began to reveal the content of his meeting, he was furious much more than normally, this time I could see his eyes turn red, after he shared all the gory details, I kind of understood his grief, but as always I wasn't the one to put nothing pass people, so really i wasn't surprised. But every so often I would play the surprise card, because he did not like it when I said I'm Not Surprised, Why Are You? He had made several undertones about me being cynical and that I had little or no trust in people, so to appease his tender heart, I would pretend i was shocked. (But in reality), I would have been shocked had those folks actually did the right thing, in my book, it wasn't in them to do right.

But nope, he still (had a hard on) so to speak) for waiting to see them show their loving, tender, humanitarian, he thy brother's keeper side. I guess i was somewhat bitter and cynical, I'm sure he was right, i did not trust people with good cause, I usually knew how it would turn out, (you know how it is, with a leopard and his stripes and all). Or maybe i had gone through enough, i had learned to see people as people and not place a value or title on them they had not rightfully earned. I could stand up in the pulpit all day and night, with scriptures spewing from my mouth, but that would not cover for the humanness of man. So, I just watched as well as prayed, something Kevin and I wasn't in agreement with, we fought loudly and brazenly about that subject. Sometimes to the point of almost no return. There were times I thought of it as touch and go.

I guess this writing thing was a massive part of the Begos Family, because his mom was just as stern about my procrastination as her son was, although she did not say anything directly, she would indirectly get me by giving me different types if writings, some she write and collections of things she and other associates produced, I guess to pluck my heart to get up and be about my calling. She wrote diligently and with pride. She was great with editorial standards. She would stop by my job and drop off little articles, those were the days I truly appreciated my new friends, she was just as intentional as her son, meek and humble.

Not like Kevin in that he pressed me, as if he knew his time with me wasn't long or that I had things to say that were long over-do. The fierceness in his persistent hammering of me, now leads me to believe he was on a mission, I think I missed out on some of the tastiest parts of his mission, because I thought I had forever. I thought he was a Journalistic Nag, but no, he wasn't, his soul knew things, our flesh could not possibly understand through the human lens. He was being himself, he was a writer first above all.

We had another terrible fight today. This time it was regarding my writing. Kevin wanted me to change my writing, to attract a wider brand of audience and i felt that the vernacular of my writing expresses who I am. And I felt as if i changed, I would be a sell out and that's just what I told him. Anyway, I truly do appreciate him and his mother they both always encourage me to speed up my writing. I have four books somewhere In between finished and could possibly be. I have one completed it is of poems. I simply stated in one of my rants that I was 100 percent sure he knew audiences, but I was 100 percent sure, i did not want to lose the reasoning behind my word.

I am afraid if I branch out to far my true meaning will get lost and the Voices would go away. But as a publisher, journalist, author and friend he wasn't having it. He stated cases and gave point. But I screamed and walked out. I can be the drama queen, I really can, well after that fight he began to not push so much, we were walking along the Russell-Fields Pier at Pier Park in Panama City, he said well Rose as stubborn as you are, is probably as right as you are. There is still room at the table for your chosen words. Although I still have reservation, I do believe an audience exist for your type writing, as did my wines. He said can you give me an off the cuff response to slavery, in the view point of a black woman. I Stopped walking, sat at the bench, closed my eyes, prayed and waited for the voice. (oh yeah, I turned on my phones voice recorder,)

There at that very moment, birth was given to:
Unwanted Seed: a poem which made its way into a

89

collection of over 400, copy written recordings in the Library of Congress Division of Copyrights. He eventually (with painful reservations) bought into the voices. Those were the spiritual essence of my being, those were the places I ventured off to when I needed to seek reality. Those were the guides who kept me abreast of the changes in other people and the effects it would have on me. There was a time, i took no heed to the voices, and those ended up being the times I failed miserably. I guess the old saying is true " when you know better you do better or the one that states: we live, and we learn. And this I have.

Sometimes I felt as if I was on stage, he would call me in the middle of the night, ask me a question, sometimes a vague question, with no depth, sand or grit. Just some off the wall stuff (I would think) as months and years passed, I learned that he was grooming my gift, he enjoyed my sense of self-worth and tenacious quality, he once said you are great, you actually just needed me to come and get you. I kind of did not know how to take that, was he assuming I was loss or not in reality. No that's not what he meant at all, he meant I was like him and that a lot of folks could not tone-down my gifts, see them or even understand them. It would take a likeminded person to say, ok Rose you could shine deeper if you stood in your own light alone, giving your glider room to grow.

(He was cool and deep like that, if he found you worthy he would come for you, he would press you, he would seek out your power source, not to abuse it, but to help you use your energy to strive and bloom).

After I had completed the poem book or had it copywritten, I posted something on Facebook pertaining to that fact, he immediately called , more excited than me, he

90

said Bravo, but it's about time, just remember when you become rich and famous, start hanging out with Tyler Perry making movies and doing guess appearance, don't forget to breathe, don't forget you left me home. I laughed and said silly rabbit, where ever I go, you will too. (I would have never thought, that would not be the case, not physically anyway) but today as i sit to write an reminisce on the loyalty of his love, kindness and approach, I now know that where ever I now go, his spirit will forever remain with me. For he was the driving force, God used to elevate and ignite my gift.

Chapter 13

Through Sickness, Health and Death

I cried every day, I prayed every day, I looked upon his fragile face, and I saw a scared man, although he tried very hard not to let me see his fear, I saw it anyway, I saw it in the glimmer of his eyes, I saw it in the words he used, when asking me questions, or making sure I remembered some of the things he had urged me to complete or accomplish, I saw it in his hugs, I saw it in his messages and the way he brought up days, nights and times we had shared. I heard it in the way he laughed, I heard it in his holding of my hand, as I sat next to his hospital bed. I knew in my heart he had changed, there was something about that sullen look, there was something about his gentle forehead kiss, there was something about his smile and his words which said, Things are going to be different.

I sat near him, my heart sadly sinking because this viral, blooming man, had a sad, weakened look on his face, and there was nothing I could do to change it. I sat there holding his hand, hoping he would use this time as a learning tool, a chance to not hold this town so close to his heart, that it destroyed him in the process, I wanted to be angry, because I needed someone to blame for the fragile man that sat before me, I wanted to cause someone else to hurt, because I was sitting there hurting, knowing I could not magically make all his sickness and sadness go away, I was so sure that he would have noticed his symptoms, had he not been so bogged down in caring about things no one else cared about.

I was so angry, so sad, so confused, so bewildered and so down right destroyed, at the prospect of possibly losing him. To be honest, I really did not think he would die, I thought god would show him his error of neglect for his own life and give him a new lease on life, I was 100 percent positive he would bounce back, and we would take all those trips he promised me. Wine vineyards, hot sauna springs, sweet grape from vines so ripened they would give you a headache from the sugar content alone. He talked about lounging in fields of flowers whom did not know they were grand, fields of leaves that changed colors in the fall, colors that shamed any Sherman Williams paint match.

He asked me if I had tasted Italian ice, the kind that was so creamy, it would melt before it actually touched your tongue. The kind that would diminish even the fancy shops on Duval Street in Key West, spices and smells that escaped the human mind and traveled into the darkest corners of my senses, while enveloping my taste buds and causing my thoughts to change. He would invite my mind on journeys such as these, he would teach my soul to travel to distant lands , while sitting on a park bench or conversing on the telephone, he could simply use the extractions of chocolate and strawberries to allow Calgon to take me away, away to places I did not think possible for my imagination or that could possibly exist in true reality.

So yes, I normally gird up my loins in anticipation of travel, he said maybe he would not run again for Mayor and we would travel, write books and see some of gods amazingly remarkable wonders. I truly deep down in my soul found his idea of travel and wonder as a time soon to come, I dreamt of the days, nights, weeks, month, the adventures trailing along with my friend, feasting on the fat of the land, the joys and wonders of high mountains, low valleys and walking through life loving it. Making sure I delved into the majestic unbelievable tastes of gods amazing splendors. I could hardly wait to taste this food, see the colors of the green grass, soak in the mountain peaks, water colors, pebbles, rocks, singing birds, smells of early spring and hot summer nights, only to return the next day and witness the same things over again.

(Oh yeah, I was ready for that, I spoke with my children, I told them that perhaps I would travel for some time, in the next couple years after his term was up, maybe depending on how he felt about his Mayoral completions. I told them that this could open me up to challenges I did not know existed), I looked over at him and I saw those things because he encouraged me to dream, dream big, touch the ceiling and soar, release my heart to the sky and my imagination to eternal bliss. And yet I sat there praying for a miracle, I even tried to make a deal with God, I said keep him, heal him, I even repented for him, I said God his heart is so big, he forgot to add himself when he was helping, so please forgive him, please give him another chance, let him live and in health and strength. Allow him to ask for what Jeremiah asked for, more time to see the goodness in the land of the living.

So I sat there holding his hand, something deep in my soul said tell him all that lives in you, so I sat up, extended my hand out to him and said Hello my name is Rose, there is nothing perfect about me, I get angry, I pout, I shut down, I raise my voice, and I am not afraid of the big bad wolf. I love hard, I laugh hard, I cry hard, I have tenacity, guts and a grip. I work hard, I fight hard and I give all I have, to those who I choose to let in. He smiled a weak smile, extended his hand and said Hello Rose, I am Kevin and I know all these things about you, that is why I linger, because I know I did not choose you only, I know you opened up for me. He said why are we meeting again? I said because I feel that every now and again, we must start fresh, leaving all the bad, negative, wrong words, unrepented requirements, unsatisfied measures, deathly drama behind and say Hello once again.

That was who we were, we renewed our friendship as I sat on his hospital bed, room 103 Weems Memorial 2021. In my heart there wasn't anything left but to move forward, he told me he would need therapy to restore his strength and I promised to take him to his therapy, he said this would sometimes be taxing to his body and to my time, but we made plans to travel this road together as friends. I never minded or gave it a second thought, as this was the very same man, who made it his business to sit with my 17 year old son and console him when he destroyed his knee and lost several chances at football scholarships at very well established colleges, I will never forget how he waltzed up to my door, all goofy smiled with something in hand, something large, tucked under his arm.

I thought it was going to be another history lesson for me, from some exotic land he had nested in, at one point of his life. He often came there with information, pictures and stories, (I loved those days, and feared them at the same time, loved them because he smiled when referring to his adventures, his smile was earth shattering, and feared them because every so often I could see his desire to roam free and my prayer was that he did not go without me). But to my surprise he had 2 cook books one with new cuisine and one with old world Authentic Recipes from every country you could imagine, he sat there next to Alex and he said I understand life has thrown you a curve, but I do not want you to give up, hold your head high, continue on, there is a light I promise.

Alex expressed how unfair it was that he could not live in the life he had planned for, all his life. He said with tears in his eyes, that as a kid, he had only wanted one thing and that was to play football and buy his mama a new house with a big kitchen, because she loved to cook. Kevin smiled and said that his grandfather was a Chef who made a very good living from his craft and that cooking or being a Chef was an awesome choice, had he considered that as a career, Alex looked at him as if he was crazy, cooking he said, no sir that had never crossed my mind ever, I'm a ball player, I'm not interested in cooking, no sir I am not. Kevin then asked me to leave the room, they talked laughed and finally the room became silent. Finally, he said Rose didn't you tell me Alex had a scholarship at GCSC for Culinary Arts, I said yes why, he smiled and said you are going to take him there to meet the Professors.

I said why? He said, because Alex will sign himself up for classes, because we have decided to not loose football, but until he heals, we are not going to waste any time, we will add Culinary as an option, any good man knows how to do more than one thing and besides my grandfather was great at it. I stood there in pure shock, I had begged, cried, pleaded, cursed, screamed, even tried to bribed Alex with a car, offered him money, I had done just about everything and pulled every trick in the book , to get that kid to respond to a different way of getting to a future and to no avail, and within an hour or so Kevin had him wanting to be a world traveling Chef, seeing all the exotic scenery and cooking for Kings and Queens, while living the dream and becoming famous and rich. I just stood there, mouth dropped to the ground.

Never have a felt so blessed than I did at that moment, my dear friend had done it again, he had found a way to use his wisdom and charm to help me help my child, this guy was top notch in my book and I thanked god for him. So, as I watched him from his chair as I sat on his hospital bed I remembered the strong viral man and I knew I was sitting next to a favor of god, a gift hidden in plain sight, a I am my brother's keeper, a new chance for me to see the goodness of the lord, in the land of the living. I decided that day, that whatever he needed as a friend, as a chauffeur, as a cook, as a team member, as a silent partner, as an onlooker, as a secret keeper, I would do and be just that no questions asked, because he was all those things and more for me.

Some days later, he leaned in and finally admitted that he may need my help in recuperating, in the beginning. I must admit, he did all he could to keep me from seeing the sickness he faced, I guess even the meekest of them has that male pride. I became so frustrated with him on many occasions, I said why are you being so stubborn stop it and let me help. On that particular day, One of his friends pulled me to the side and said, he loves you and as a man loves a woman, he doesn't want you to see his weakened side, he wants to always look strong in your eyes, again I became upset, because I thought, doesn't he know I would not leave, hadn't our friendship grown enough, to a place where he could trust my loyalty to the game? His friend looked at me after hearing this and said, you are missing the point.

He is a man, you are a woman and we men have this stupid pride, which tells him to be strong for you, I froze! Because at that point, a flash back of his voice entered my mind. I heard his voice from almost three years ago, as it told me the secret of his confusion and reluctance, when it came to friendships, because they always ended, he was so afraid of losing people he loved, he hated death, he hated sickness, he hated a weak man. He thought that strong men were designed to be of good cheer and carry the load, that was the reason he works so hard, to be a provider and to understand the world, thereby passing the message of peace and harmony on to all he touched.

I don't think I will ever eat a duck fries again, that was one of the last things we shared while sitting on his hospital bed, he loved those things. He mostly loved food that wasn't that good for his heart, but I guess he had determined to at least eat some of the stuff that made him feel good. We sat there eating it talking about the Tap Room and Melvin as the King of Gumbo, Kevin loved that gumbo, and, in his mind, he was sure Melvin made it especially for him. Sitting there making future plans and watching the color come back to his face, seeing the desire and a glimpse of belief.

A belief that he would live, a belief that he could return to his post as mayor and as the viral happy funny motivated man he had been. I saw a hint of peace creep through his dim lens, the lens that had formally looked as if he was giving up, I saw Kevin healing, perhaps I saw what my heart wanted to see, I saw what I needed to see, so that I could rest in my heart, if I was being honest I hadn't had a lot of sleep since he had become ill, I hadn't had a lot of peace or belief, I prayed and I prayed, on some days I felt hope and on others I felt doomed, doomed to live without my friend and confidant

The perfect example is when my cousin Keenan was murdered, Kevin sat with me for hours. A couple days later he asked me if I thought my uncle and aunt would receive a visit from him. I said I'm sure they would. He said ok set it up and no you cannot come with me, I want to feel their hearts, maybe they wanna talk about things al0ne. Although I do not have kids, I would like to sit with them and understand their pain. That was Kevin, he had compassion and respected others privacy. I never told him, but my family shared all information. My aunt and uncle told me about his pleasantries, she said he cried, while telling them how sorry he was.

Also stating as he walked away, if there is anything I can do as leader of the City and Friend of Rose I will. My aunt said; I really do like him, my uncle closed it out by saying that Kevin was a great man, he shook his head and he also said they are going to run all over him, because he is too nice. He and lady Jane his mother came to the funeral, she said she felt like she was in Georgia again. Mrs. Jane related a lot of our African American things to her upbringing in Georgia. I never delved into it, I usually just smile and let her reminisce each time her mind brought her back to her young woman hood.

Chapter 14

The Tears of Remembrance

Grief is an ugly, hateful, constant ping, which consumes your inner being, grips your senses and assume possession of your life. Grief destroys the sweet taste in your mouth, Grief adds dark circles under your eyes, Grief causes you to sit in a room with one hundred people talking and you never hear one word. Grief will walk up to you, snatch the smile and sunshine out of your life and never care what you think, Grief provides no relief, Grief offers no hope, Grief gives no closure date and no heartfelt hugs.

A month has passed since your death, I finally found the strength to ride pass your house, praying that as I passed I would see a window open and you sitting, reading or planning your new plan of attack, on some of those ungrateful people you serve. Perhaps I would have come inside, perhaps we would banter back and forth about nothing, but about something, nonetheless. Perhaps you would do your usual greeting that began with how is the kids? What did you cook, how was work? None of those things happened, the silent cold stillness sat on your front porch and gruesomely waved at me, it waved anger, sadness, loneliness, blues, turmoil, desperation, unbelief and fear.

The chills of fear mixed with still a deeply painful mistrust of what was happening in my life. As I reached the corner I truly hoped, as I looked back in my rearview mirror you would be standing on the porch, beckoning me to return, as you had done so many times before. Again, my heart skipped a beat of sadness, because there was no you, no beckoning, no conversation, no laughter and no joy. Again, today I called your name, as I walked pass your photo. That smile. Those eyes, that boyish grin so real, so unmatchable, so generous and so gone. I shook off my desire to climb in my bed, cover my head and drift away, those would be self-defeating mechanisms, something you truly disliked.

I saw your spirit at the Apalachicola Farmers Market on last Saturday. Two young girls gave me a lesson in true, new and complete friendship, they displayed the ability to meet someone and go the extra mile for them. Something I had watched you do so many times. The one young girl stated with boldness that she had found her truest and best friend, she stated that this was her first friend, and that's how I feel about you, until you, who accepted me without reservations, with a gleeful look every time I appeared, someone who wanted to sit near me, someone who would call just to say hello, someone who wanted nothing from me, but wanted everything in me. The young lady had boldly appeared and pronounced her intent to see that her friend was happy and would do whatever it took to see that this happened. That was you, I saw you, I smiled and said out loud, Kevin would be so happy and proud now.

Your intentions toward the farmers market was that it became a wellness place, a place senior and families with kids could get vegetables and fruits, healthy items that would supply their families nutritional needs. I can't lie, I really did not want to manage that market, I fought you tooth and nail. But finally, you won, as you so often did. Today I am very grateful you pushed me pass my thoughts on that subject, I have learned so much about people and I'm sure you knew it all along, but I adore being there, who would have ever thought the farmers market in tiny Apalachicola would carry so many stories, so much love, so many memories, I guess you knew.

As I walked into your house today, I smelt your scent, as if you were standing there, your home was warm, so inviting and full of life. as I walked from room to room talking to your mother, I could feel your breath on the back of my neck, as if your presence was still alive and moving. If I did not know better I would say you were still here, with blood running warm in your veins. I felt safe, I did not feel that absence nor did I feel afraid.

The weather was bad today Tropical Storm Fred, I missed seeing you run around town like a father hen trying to save his children. The look of stress as it penetrated your brows, in anticipation of how safe your citizens would be, could be or should be.
I thought about how aggressively you would be moving about, riding up and down checking roads, looking down alley ways, calling me hoping that all the senior's citizens had food, lights and a safe place to battle this storm. These are the times I'm sure a lot of folks will miss you, I knew

exactly how much time and effort you place with and put into the lives of the aged.

Alive and Alone

The heart beats as the blood rush's through my body, I breathe, I laugh, I walk, i talk, I work, I dream, I write, I sing in the shower, I have an opinion and i think.

I think about the noise in my chest, i think about the loud in my head, and yet there is an eerie pain of silence everywhere. I smile as I walk into a room, there are tons of people everywhere

They say hello, they walk around in front of me, behind me, above me, beneath me, beside me and yet the silence still has a bitter taste of aloneness, not of calm peace, but of massive grief

The touch, the smell, the encounters, the engagements, the party's, the meets, greets and treats, the getaways, the boats and the yachts are but silent tokens of being there, they are not tokens of living there.

The false smiles, fake conversations, the unanswered questions, the wait for a while, the I will let you know, the maybes and the perhaps, are all voices of negative, neglectful truths and alive lies

I notice them because they are visible to my invisible prance through this life, unwavering, unconscious, undiluted, unintentional and unnecessary, but there they are standing in the shadows.

They never see me, it doesn't matter my dance, prance or stance, I am never suspected as the one, therefore I can violated the order because no one watches me

No one ever would imagines I had the answer or knew the right question, because they assume I am not there, that I am merely a shadow or reflection of something they invented or allowed.

When in truth, I manufactured the entire thing, my arms stretch farther and wider than the visible eye or deepest dream, I laugh quietly because I wonder when will they see the mirror

Maybe never or maybe today who will ever know, it's painful to be alive and alone, it's as if one is sitting on the seat of hope, while everyone kneels before the seat asking for help, but never looking up to see hope staring right back at them

It is as if there is a feather in your hand, but instead we chase birds all day and night, hoping to catch one and pluck one out, it is as if the sun shines to brighten your day and you stay inside

It is as if I said I love you and you call the psychic to see if she can direct you to it, we sometimes stand in wait under the shadow for the answer, with our eyes closed, hoping the shadow will find us.

Such a terrible mundane existence to be alive and locked in our own alone. While people knock at our door to say hello.

This is what I wrote as I sat in front of your house wishing you were there, I had a pain inside my chest that appeared to fall into a coma, regardless to how much i prayed, cried or pretended to smile, the pain would not wake up and walk away, **By Rose Griffin**

Getting to know him was a challenge, all our days were not peachy, some days or night he got on my damn nerves. He would cling to stuff that I had assumed he should have let go of and his desire was for me to cling right along with him and I had no intentions on doing that, I had done so much therapy and spiritual work on myself, and to indulge in those action would be self-defeating, and I said those exact words, well that did not go over well, he wasn't one who wanted to deal with issues, he wanted to fix something, plant a vegetable or hide in the house and pout until it went away. And that wasn't my new way of life, of course there have been periods of my life where I chose those mechanisms of digression, but no sir, not now I was long pass that.

But not Kevin,

in all his well-meaning heart wrenching love for life and people he still had not conquered dealing with his issues, he had sat with monks, he had visited an ayahuasca retreat for restoration and rejuvenation, he prayed and meditated in some of the biosphere's most exotic retreats and yet there was a place inside of him that was still broken. And it all stemmed from some deep dark secrets, that will forever rest in my soul, because it was left with me in confidence. I think that was part of the reason I never walked away, although he did push my buttons on several occasions to a point where I assumed, it would be easier to just cash in my chips and walk away from the table.

Speaking of chips and table, he nor I were gamblers, but we had decided to visit the Casino in Mississippi, we sat there and planned to pull slots, play cards, eat good, take pictures for his I've done that book, so we set out to do an adventure, mostly because so many people on face book had bragged about their casino trips, he wanted to feel the hype. The drive was good, he drove, I drove, we laughed talked ate food and sang songs, well he sang, I just "murdered the hits", because everyone knows I can't carry a tune, even if it is in a bucket.

After registering in the Beau Rivage Resort and Casino, we retreated to our rooms, this guy wanted a king size bed for his room and I a queen for mine, he said if he was going to be there he may as well take full advantage of the amenities, And that we did. He had already investigated the massage set up, that was the first thing he said, ok it's massage time, so off we went, although I found it refreshing, he had an in between notion about it, not that it wasn't refreshing, but seeing that he had lavished in mud baths, sauna, sweat rooms and deep tissue messages, this was a far cry from what he was use too and me being not so well versed in the art of massage therapy, at that time I had no idea how deep, those therapeutic measures could go.

From there he wanted to see the beach, so we walked and he told me about his dream he constantly had to walk on water, not as if he was Jesus, but as a point of meditation, being so intertwined with the earth and its powers that he actually could levitate, where he had surrendered all of him and that his soul would soar and flow with the earth's vibrations. Up the road from the beach was (old Spanish mansions, he said were established when the early invasions happened. No, they were not plantations. They were actual homes of Spanish settlers, who had set up camp prior to the plantation group.

We found a charming cast iron Lighthouse on Biloxi's Beach Blvd. I swear he leaped in glee, he acted as if he had caught the trifecta at the craps table. The 57 spiral steps wore me out, but not Kevin, he loved it, something changed for him as he maneuvered his way up toward the sky, he smiled, his voice raised to a gleeful pitch. This lighthouse was the magnetic energy needed to revive him from the stress of his job. Something to wash away the blues, I now can understand why he continue to work at St George Island's Lighthouse, his peace was inside those walls.

Those were the levels of education I acquired while being Kevin's friend. He loved knowledge and he reveled in the knowledge that those around him were just as astute as him, he was never the type to want to be the guy who knew it all, he believed in corporate sharing and corporate learning, he felt that in that way, no one was left behind and each of us had the same opportunity.

He carried a glimmer in his eye a sort of prideful glimmer, the kind I often saw when his educational side surfaced. I remember the day I learned about his Percy Sledge knowledge, we were riding alone and When a Man Loves a Woman come on the radio, he hummed a few notes, then he sharply said, that guy was amazing, he loved life, he had 12 children not all by the same woman of course(that's a lot of kids for one woman to carry), and three of his kids followed in his footsteps as musically inclined individuals. That boyish matter of fact twinkle surfaced and just like that it was gone. He did not continue the educational piece, he just kept driving and I kept smiling, because I loved those moments.

Now back to the casino we went, showered, dressed and headed to the gambling table, (well almost) we found ourselves distracted by a live band with Jamaican sounds, so I guess you all know where we ended up. Yep sitting at a table listening to sound and eating Cajun Shrimp Tacos, he had beer and i had sprite and cranberry juice with cherries, we sat there for 3 hours, laughing watching the crowd. We actually did do some betting, but it did not happen at the gambling table or slot machines, it actually happened while sitting at that table, in that very room, observing the massive crowd and deciding who would get the drunkest of them all, who would fall flat on their face, while making moves on the dance floor.

Who would dance the raunchiest, who would be pulled from the floor by their spouse, girl friend or boyfriend...I actually won most of the bets, because although he didn't like to admit it, but I was better at reading folks than he was. It was a very fun trip and it lasted only a day and a half from Friday mid-day and back home by Sunday morning I was so very glad we took that trip, within the next few days I could see his relaxation numbers going up and he walked a little lighter, he said he slept well at least for a few nights after our return. Which was an incredible feat, seeing that he never slept.

Just in time for me to get dressed and head off to church and speaking of church, he called me one night and said Rose what is the name of your church? I told him Friendship Missionary Baptist Church, under the leadership of Pastor James Williams, he then said, do they welcome guess, I said of course anyone at any time, come as you are, love and a welcome spirit is always abounding. I said why, are you coming? he said yes. That meant a great deal to me, seeing that he was subject to the ideals of his upbringing and former Christian style choices. I said you're such a great guy, he laughed and said yep I know.

Chapter 15

Thinking Out Loud:

Death of a loved one can remove the sweetness from your mouth. It can bring bitterness to and from your heart. Pain of grief is destructive to your inner voice.

When an informed person dies, it is as if a dictionary, or an entire world of knowledge leaves, unless someone has taken the time to read from those books. You will never know the knowledge you lose along the way

I was a mess, I was falling apart, right before everyone and nobody noticed, I sent out smoke signals, but nobody noticed. Everybody was busy living. I am very good at pretending I guess. I worked at it, I had a somewhat good poker face or maybe it just did not register to anyone, that I might just be in need, I don't know how or why, but somehow, I always found myself connected to the needy and greedy (I guess that is another thing Kevin and I had in common). Those who couldn't see pass their needs. But yes I was sinking fast and hard, yet when my phone rang it was never a how are you, it sounded something like " ohhhhhh poooor pitiful them", anyway I was headed straight for the' sad sack farm'.

That is why I miss you mostly because you saw me, you heard me and you cherished my intent.

As I sat here thinking on all these deaths, Covid Covid Covid everywhere. I think of all the things you had done, to keep this city away from the pestilence of that plague and how shortly after your passing, the town seemed to have been turned over to the perils of death.

This would have surely as I'm breathing, given you a heart attack, it would have sent you into the deepest darkest depression of your entire life.

My heart continues to revert back to a bible scripture that says: That the prayers of the righteous availed much, so, what if the righteous prayers died with them, what if the one standing in the gap with a pure heart was no more... what if what stood between God's wrath, was Kevin's desire and warm heart for the city. Wow what if...

He was not a pet owning guy. Although he liked the ones his mom had, you probably would have never seen him walking a dog or belly scratching a cat, something to do with not having time for those things, just as he didn't or hadn't found the time to cultivate a family. On several occasion he talked about wishing he had placed his face toward kids and leaving a legacy for them, he said those were the inner desires he dare not dream of at his age. He shook his head took a deep breath of sigh, I also had studied him long enough to know that his sigh meant, those were the things he regretted the most.

112

I Missed A Lot!!!!!!!

I truly must admit, I slipped in my approach toward Kevin, because I had assumed he would be around for the next 30 to 40 years, I did not ask him some of the things i should have, I did not delve deep enough, as I sit today typing out my heart, I realized there were a few more things I needed to know, there were a few more ideas I wanted to share and a few more questions only he could have answered. I hurt now when I think of the color yellow, I never asked him why he like it so much and what did it mean when he would stare at me without saying a word or why old people owned his heart. I chalked it all up to a simple saying" oh that's just who Kevin is he loves people" but suppose it went deeper than that, suppose he was planting seed that would one day be his legacy, we talked about many things, but never his legacy, as I write, It may sound as if I have him all figured out, but honestly there were chapters (whole books) inside of him, I will never know about. Perhaps that will serve me well in my ignorance is bliss stage, or maybe I knew enough to know he wasn't ordinary, but more on the lines of extraordinary.

I sit frustrated, because now that he's gone, I desire one more conversation, I have a list of question, questions I thought would be useful when we were in our eighties, old bored and needed some topic to keep us laughing.

I don't know if I ever kissed him good enough, I don't know if i held his hand tight enough, I don't know if I cried with him long enough, I don't know if a listened contently enough, I thought that I would have more time for those questions and answers.

113

A few months before he died I had begun watching a television show called Drop Dead Diva, it was a show about someone dying and returning to life in another body with another life. Well shortly after Kevin passed. I found myself looking at every stranger that crossed my path, looking for signs, looking for a smile, looking at their eyes, looking at their speech, searching out each word, trying to hear his voice wondering who he came back as, and would I know him, or would I like the new him. I truly wanted art to imitate life and he would return, well you all know the answer to that question, it was only wishful thinking.

Those were some of the worse days of my life, I lived in torturous times of my grief, I struggled to promote peace in my damaged soul.

Are you sending me messages?
I turned on the radio and Marvin Gaye and Tammy Terrell was singing "Ain't No Mountain High Enough (one of your favorite songs)", I sat there, another trigger for my dampened soul. Memory lane threw me another curve ball, I saw your face as we drove along any given highway, singing that song so many times. I walked into a store later that night and I heard Keith Urban and Carrie Underwood singing "The Fighter" (my favorite song) So I guess this is your way of being my drop-dead diva tv show... your spirit bringing me familiar sounds...

His fascination with science had no boundaries, he had full intent to delve into the mitochondria DNA of African American women, I sat with him hours on end, listening to his ideas and writing out his plans, for the reintroduction of the fascinating fact that only African American woman were the only species with the ability to create any variation of any other human, no other women had been given that God given ability to do this. His question is why

114

only us, I was very willing to be the subject of study, because to study this or learn the answer to this question, would instill an extra amount of pride for myself as an African American Woman.

So, I freely engaged him on every turn. Kevin the Scientist never ceased to amaze me. He was always delving into the unknown, the trickier the answer more intrigued he became, with the subject, I often thought that was his attraction to me, I was never the simple one, more like the complicated onion with tons of layers, different curve, ridge, scents and the ability to (play spade without giving away my card game). Anyway, one could never say from one day till the next, what Mr. Begos was thinking or planning.

To be honest sometimes it became downright scary, he was humble but he had a Dr Jekyll and Mr. Hyde side in him, he commonly did not use subjects of flesh, but I've sat back in my little corner and watched him use his physiological, psychological, Scientific as well as his journalistic skills to work folks, whom actually thought they were in control or as the term in slang language goes, they thought they were truly "running shit".

Well it's October 10th my Cancer Free Birthday, this would have been a celebration date for us, you would have gotten me a pink cake, some sparkling drink and loads of Chinese Food(shrimp lo mein, sautéed vegetables, peanut chicken, brown sauce broccoli and those crazy fortune cookies from Hong Kong Bistro, right there in Apalachicola We would have sat on the floor in your living room and celebrated my life as we had done in the past three years. Thank you, Kevin, for cherishing my life, it's really impressive how we gain love for ourselves, at the hand of the love others sometimes give us.

Chapter 16
Fortune Cookies

A well rounded astute business man, public speaker, science, journalist, world traveler, entrepreneurs, with the resounding abilities of accurate predictions and scientific proof, the intuitiveness and pizazz to overturn the debt ratio of the City of Apalachicola and yet he believed in fortune cookies. He possessed tons of those things, he kept everyone he had ever received, and oftentimes would leave them in places, where others would find them, (as if he was a fairy dropping golden dust along the way as he moved through this earth) giving those who found them, the opportunity to dream big... or at least gather a smile upon their faces... he loved smiles.

He told me that my smile opened doors. He then went on to say, someone would need to study me, in order to discover whether it was a smile or a smirk. He also stated with matter of fact-ness, that a less worthy opponent, would do well to learn the difference. I think in that arena we matched, because there were times, I would watch his interactions with others and think silently, you people better back off, that's his I'll get you back smirk, which in itself looked like a smile. It was such a pleasure to have learned his inner thoughts through his facial expressions. But as he stated one would have served themselves better, had they known the inner workings of his smile.

In my eyesight and mindset, Kevin was the creative genius of God's design, his talents, gifts, patience and forgiveness were a direct flashing signal of how God loves, cherishes and protects us. The interior of his being was in direct correlation to "thy brothers' keepers' syndrome". Which became evident with each passing moment of compassion he showed, despite the tumultuous intimidation and stone-cold rejection he faced at the hands of other, but he rose, and yet he smiled and yet he continued the road to progress our City into a stage of dignity, despite being forced to entertain the whims of the wicked.

A couple days before he died, he was in 7th heaven, his cheer was up and he felt so please with his prognosis, he had been given the all clear, the doctors had advised him, and stated that the infections were all gone and that he could go home on Friday. I then said GREAT, but I shall not come there on Friday, I will leave that time to you and your mother and sister to talk business or set some things in order. I will be there on Saturday I promise. He said if that is what you want, ok but make sure you are there on Saturday, there are things I will need from you. I agreed, while thinking, what does he want now? he oftentimes left the conversations and myself in a vague state of mind.

Well Saturday I did sit there, but it wasn't because we were smiling, hugging or with a note pad taking instructions on his needs for the physical, I sat there with his sister and Karen, trying to figure out how to bury him and all the details that went along with the dead. Yes Dead, My Beloved Kevin was dead, yes, he did leave the hospital on Friday and yes, I did come to his house on Saturday. Those words echo in my heart late at night, early in the morning, whilst I drove down the highway, and I thought, why did I not know, how could I have not seen and what else should I have done.

    Perhaps had I known, I would have held his hand tighter, kissed his forehead harder, told him how much I loved and appreciated all his kindness, how much I thanked god for his presence in mine and my children lives, how often I watched his grace and peaceful spirit and thought what a great man he was, I would have hissed his lips and said thank you for showing love, even when none was returned or Farewell my Champion of the People, I would have laid beside him one more time and whispered a poem in his ear, I would have poured him some Mango Punch or baked him some Brisket, I would have never left his side, I would have stayed there until the bitter end. I know he knew these things, but I would have said them anyway.

118

Chapter 17

Juniper Tree

Kevin love Shell Point, he said the peace there was unmatchable, the quiet tone, he said he could think clearly in that atmosphere. We would spend hours just sitting by the water, sometimes we would pull out the chairs and sit under the gazebo. But to be honest his love centered around the Juniper Tree. Which stood on a hill near the gazebo, he said it reminded him of the one mentioned in the bible: in association to Jobs (in the bible)Juniper Roots as used as a parasitic food based item or medicinal support,(yep that was Kevin the scientist who told me this) As we sat under the juniper tree he made mention of the tree, , Not only did he give reference to job, he also made mention that the Canaanites saw this tree as symbolic of the fertility goddess Ashera. I could not let him out do me in theological knowledge, so I chimed in with; that very same brand of tree, hosted the Prophet Elijah as he hid from Queen Jezebels wrath. He smiled shook his head and said of course but are you going to dismiss the Canaanites and their fertility goddess?

I said no sir I am not ignoring her, so I stood to my feet, took up my chair and moved away from that tree. He said where are you going? and I turned dropped my chair, put my hands on my hips and stated; Ashera and her Canaanites can have their fertility goddess, their juniper tree, and their shade, I am going under the gazebo, I want nothing to do with her fertility…. He screamed in laughter, until he turned beet red, I think I made his day, wasn't that often freedom rose up inside of him, but it did that day.

Chapter 18

My Breaking Point

I became angry today, I decided to clean my bedroom, something i hadn't done since he died. While forcing myself to rejoin reality, I pulled a box from underneath my bed, it was my when we travel box, it had oils, perfumes, first aid kit, earth medicine book, lotions, repellents, fragrances from near and far. They were supposed to accompany us on our trips, I had planned on making the most of each adventure. You spoke of deserted places of peace and quiet, also of places of sensual sounds, tunes to pierce the heart and soul. Morocco was on that list. The ABC Islands too. Anyway, as I opened the box,

I accidentally dropped one of the bottles and it spilled oil everywhere, I pressed my hand in the oil and placed the hand to my nose and I cried, I sat on the floor and opened all the bottles, pouring them out on the floor (because why not, there was no reason to save them anymore, my trips were not going to happen, well not with you that is) and immediately I cried. I cried so sad, I wept, I sank again and again deeper to the floor, finally I sat there, finally it hit me, oh my God he's gone. As if a 50-ton brick slapped me in the chest, I sat there beside my bed hugging a bottle of oil, squeezing it for life, the scent vibrated through my soul... a damn bottle of oil, wow I'm a freaking mess... "a damn bottle of oil". Really Rose, you let the oil win????

Chapter 19

Goodbye

I have been mourning a loss, I've mourned it in public, secretly or shall I say invisibly. Should I let my hellos also stand for my goodbyes. Because it seems as if I never get a goodbye
I wonder sometimes, people have always died away from me. Even back when I was a young girl working as a nursing assistant, I would grow fond of old people, they would be joyous and happy one day. I would show up the next day and they would be dead, gone no goodbyes. I hate the action of no goodbyes. If I could change anything in this World, it would be the right for people to get a proper goodbye, a reasoning out of respect, anything that would soothe the heart of man/woman.

I believe in my soul that if we as humans could have that, we would be better prepared to face anything, not a "goodbye I'm dying tomorrow at two pm". But a special set moment that came before death, a week, a day even a year just a point in time that was worth looking back on, cherishing the loss and a place of peace to cushion the pain. That's what I desire.

Thank you, Kevin, for all the time you spent cultivating my gift and chiseling my craft. I know, sometimes I frustrated you, with my firm will and bold stance, my unyielding need to do it always my way and to not budge an inch, especially when my soul felt as if I was right. I know it was sometimes painstaking to stare in the face of stubbornness, but now after all the years and many months, I can close my eyes, see your face and do this for us.

Chapter 20

The Final Ride

You once said, for a man to have traveled around the world from city to city, state to state, country to country, you had never walked through Disney World for fun. You said you had walked the streets of Crete Greece, hung out and eaten in their fancy taverns, browsed through the most incredible museums and yet you had never eaten ice cream while riding a carousel, I said neither had I, I have spent time holding baby bags while my kids played on rides or spun around on the Carousel while keeping a child afloat. But never had I spent time with or for Rose. We both agreed that we should have and would someday soon, we made plans to walk through Disney eating ice cream and singing.

It now appears that your death has hindered decades of things we had set our heart to complete. It seems as if your death made a mockery of our future, it seems as if your death rules out my laugher and some of your joy, it seems as if your death, turned our sunny days into dark sad nights. I mourn our future and our plans, I mourn the passing of the life we thought we finally had found, I mourn the passing to the end of our late-night conversations and get away, I mourn the passing of our secret sharing and heartfelt trust. I sit here and mourn.

Believe it or not I went to Disney and I took your picture with me, my main goal was to settle somethings for you and I, I walked up to the carousel and got on a pretty horse, while waiting for the man to start the ride, I took your picture out of my wallet, held it tightly in my hand, closed my eyes and said ok Kevin we are here we will ride, no weapon formed against us shall prosper. And as the carousel circled the park so did my tears circled my face, not because of sadness but because I felt that I had held true to one of our plans, I so hope you were happy as we rode around, as I waved to all the on lookers, I was saying Kevin said hello and so does Rose. I then walked proudly over to the Tea Cups, stood in line, (while wiping small tears from my eyes) waiting on my turn, I sat down and squeezed your photo again,(still gripped tightly in the clutches of my determined heart) as I spun around, I thought of how much fun it would have been to see your beautiful face all shiny as you took your ride.

As I stepped out of that ride, I took a deep breath, I felt accomplished, I felt alive, I felt as if you were there and all was well, I eventually went to sit on a bench alone, so that I could speak with you, I silently whispered, I hope you are having fun, I hope the kid inside you, is screaming screams of glee, I hope the energy I'm feeling around me right now, is your laughter, as I licked the ice cream that rolled down my arm from the cone, I could hear your voice say, I bet that taste good?.

This trip was a complete surprise, and it was all in part to Mrs. Diane Duncan who surprised us girls with a get-away, I had no idea it would be their 5oth Anniversary and this I would find peace, that I would laugh or that you and I would take the final ride of our beings, although you will never be far away from my soul. I exhaled as I walked through that park, I saw your smile, I saw your eyes glisten,

I saw your cheeks expand, as they so often did, when your joyous peace reached its peak. I heard your voice saying; hold your head up, we are here now enjoy it, I am depending on you to carry us forward, I am depending on you to keep the dream alive, I am depending on you to never let them forget.

I sat in the Amway Center on Church Street in Orlando Florida and I took a deep breath, not really sure if I had found permission in my soul, to enjoy life again. I knew I wanted to start on mine and Kevin's bucket list, but I wasn't sure if life would let me proceed or if my depression would subside long enough to get the full effects of why I was there, I tried to smile, lord knows I was grateful for Mrs. Diane's gesture of love, lord knows I put the best on the outside and walked, talked and made jokes, as if the old Rose was sitting in that seat, as if I had it all together, no one asked me if I was hurting, so I said nothing either.

Anyway, as I sat there, I prayed please lord give me strength not to walk away still 100% damaged, if you could just break it in half, I will forever be grateful. I pressed my lips close together as I often did when I was searching for strength and suddenly, a Husband and Wife duo called: The War and Treaty hit the stage(the opening act in Lauren Daigle's 2021 tour)and said Emmanuel, "I lay down my everything" and so I did, I laid down my grief, as I sat high up in the Center I felt high enough and yet low enough, to pray. And then I prayed, and I cried, I prayed again, and I cried again. I sat there for hours, as each song penetrated my soul and washed away my blues. Although there were hundreds of people in the Stadium, I felt all alone with god and the spirit of Kevin.

I saw you last night in my dream, you finally showed up. I've been waiting for you, I hoped you would come, I needed to see your face, I needed to know if you were ok. I needed to say goodbye. Not goodbye your pictures are coming down from my wall, or goodbye I won't ride pass your house again, nor goodbye, as if I won't speak your name again. But goodbye to the lost soul I carry around. Thank you for the silent smile and the gentle nudge in peace direction.

I wanted to taste his mouth, not for a kiss, but to inhale his words, because his soul fascinated me.

By Rose Griffin.....

Adieu Mon Ami

Well Kevin I am doing as I promised, I will never let them forget you, so I have decided to release these words, I hope they are pleasing to you. I send the hope of longevity and pleasure toward this book as it is truly designed for the world to know the man I know. Put a good word in, make sure these words reach the right hands, ask our God to use these words to bring peace in the hearts of those who loved you and understanding to those who did not know or understand you.

This has been a painful journey, dredging up all these memories inside my mind and heart. I have cried tears for my dear friend, his mother, his dear sister and countless of co-workers and cousins. I thought about not publishing, I told myself if I told them about him, I would lose the private parts of him and I fashioned my thought with the premise that, if I knew parts of him no one else knew, I could keep him just for me." How Selfish".

About the Author

Rose M Griffin is a previously published author "Ready for the Wedding, not prepared for the Marriage", she is a mother, grandmother, she has studied Addictions Counseling and Psychology, earning several licenses and degrees in those fields, along with her establishing of Understand Inc Advocacy Center and Bent Isn't Broken, these Non Profits (501c-3), serves as beacons to numerous needy families, along with many single males and females in search of clarity in the age of brokenness. She is most passionately about her work in her church ministry.

.

Acknowledgements Of Use:

Kevin Begos: Tasting the Past and Against their Will

Acknowledgement on the KJV of the bible and the use of partial scriptures

Acknowledgment of use of all Restaurants, names, owners and any use of their names

Acknowledgement on any use of words or phrases associated to any person, place or thing

Book Information and Details

Copyright Date: September 28, 2021

Isbn- 13
979-8-9878745-0-9

Publishing Company
Upton Turrell Publishing
398 24th Avenue # 505
Apalachicola Florida 32320

Made in the USA
Columbia, SC
14 August 2023

21609447R00075